From Ann's Kitchen

The Recipes and Reminiscences of Ann Sorrentino

A Treasury of Italian Ethnic Cuisine

by Ann Sorrentino

Published by Bordighera and Fra Noi

Staff

Publishers	Bordighera Inc./Fra Noi Inc.
Senior Editor/Project Coordinator	Paul Basile
Editor	Dolores Sorrentino
Typesetting/Layout/Design/Illustrations	Mary Racila
Copy/Index Editor	Paula Perkins
English Proofreader	Rosanne Cataldo
Italian Consultant	Dr. Giuliana Castellani Koch
Office Manager	Marie Gallo
Publishing Consultant	Dr. Anthony Tamburri
Cover Photograph	Jerry Daliege
Ceramics for Photograph	Tutti Italia
	700 N. Michigan Ave. • 4th Floor • Chicago, Ill. 60611
	312-951-0510
Four-Color Separations	Tukaiz Communications
	2917 N. Latoria Lane • Franklin Park, Ill. 60131
	800-543-2674
Printer	Jumbo Jack's Cookbooks
	301 Broadway • P.O. Box 247 • Audubon, Iowa 50025
	800-798-2635
Computer and Design Consulting	cj graphic solutions inc.
	221 E. Division St. • Villa Park, Ill. 60181
	630-530-0578

Library of Congress Cataloging-in-Publication Data

Sorrentino, Ann, 1917-
   From Ann's Kitchen : the recipes and reminiscences of Ann
Sorrentino : a treasury of Italian ethnic cuisine / by Ann
Sorrentino.
      p.   cm.
   Includes index.
   ISBN 1-884419-14-3
   1. Cookery, Italian.   I. Title
TX723.S656   1997
641.5945--dc21

97-43601
CIP

Prefazione
Preface

For many years my mother, Ann Sorrentino, wrote a food column for the Chicago-based Italian-American newspaper, Fra Noi. Her column reflected a diverse range of cooking styles representing the 20 regions of Italy. In addition, the column often included recipes submitted by her readers.

This collection, "From Ann's Kitchen," is a very personal one representing the foods and flavors that emanated from my mother's own amazing kitchen. Many of the recipes she served her family and guests were her own creations. Others were handed down from her Sicilian mother and grandmothers. In addition, she would sometimes add to her repertoire recipes shared by other family members and *compare*. A few of these are sprinkled throughout this collection, with sources duly noted.

The concept of a cookbook had been part of Mom's thinking for many years. She made it her mission to measure out and write down old family recipes from her childhood. If she created a new dish, she made sure to commit it to paper. She also recorded her own memories of growing up Italian in Chicago, especially recollections of food customs and holiday celebrations.

At the time of her death in 1996, her dream of a cookbook had not been completely realized, but looking among her papers I could see that the groundwork was firmly laid.

The task of compiling and editing my mother's words and personal recipes has been, of course, a labor of love. It has also been a humbling undertaking, with the sense of responsibility for correctly presenting her work never far from my mind. Please note that any errors or omissions are mine and not hers.

— Dolores Sorrentino

Ringraziamenti
Acknowledgments

I must begin these acknowledgments as I know my mother would have: by thanking her parents, Leonardo and Providenza Sodaro, and her grandparents, Andrea and Christina Sodaro, as well as her brothers and sisters, aunts and uncles, and cousins. They were a particularly close family, among whom she learned a true appreciation of food and the love that surrounds those who share it.

When she married my father, Anthony Sorrentino, in 1939, they were able to translate that love into a devotion for each other and a dedication to their family. I know she would acknowledge him as her life's greatest blessing.

Although my mother left behind the recipes and memories recorded here, this book would not exist without the vision and dedication of Paul Basile, editor of Fra Noi. He proposed the project and saw it through with tireless attention to detail. Our family is greatly indebted to Paul, Mary Racila, and the rest of the staff, whose skill, knowledge and talent gave life to these pages. A debt of gratitude is also owed to Joan Liffring-Zug Bourret of Penfield Press and Dr. Gaetano Cipolla of Arba Sicula for their kind help and cooperation.

A special thanks to those cooks who were so generous in sharing recipes that appear herein: Josephine Lucatorto and her sister, Molly Ferrari; Angela Giunta; the late Nella Scalise; Marge Tolitano; Tena Amico and her mother, the late Grace Licata; Prudence Dispensa; Linda Baron; my mother's cousin, the late Augusta Dugo; and her aunts, Carmela Sodaro and Anna Ragona.

A caring touch was added to this endeavor by a dear friend, Dr. Giuliana Castellani Koch, who graciously agreed to authenticate the Italian titles that appear above each recipe. Mille grazie, Giuliana.

I wish to express my undying gratitude to those special family members and friends who have been my loving support system from beginning to end. A very special thank you to my husband, Jim Sennebogen, for his love and unwavering patience and to the many others who have been there for tasting and testing, sharing memories and tracking down recipes. These include my Dad; my sister Patricia and brother Bob, and their families; my dear cousin, Marie Massicotte (on whom I depended over and over); my loving friends Linda Baron, Gilly Parker and Maureen Salene; and family members Tony Sodaro and Jackie Bose.

And, most especially, thank you, Mom, for everything.

— *Dolores Sorrentino*

Indice
Table of Contents

Ann Sorrentino

might be a dish of cooked greens or a few potatoes, diced and made into a delicious saffron soup. When eggs were plentiful, one egg per person would be poached in the soup. Sometimes the eggs would be poached in a delicious tomato sauce, then enjoyed with a thick slice of bread. Fresh fruit and homemade wine were always available as a sweet ending to these simple meals.

In those days, entertainment was centered in the home among family members and friends. The best of times were had during festivals and celebrations, holy days and holidays that marched through the calendar year with comforting regularity. I treasure early memories of coming home from school to find my grandmother, mother and aunt deeply involved in preparation for the next festive occasion. These preparations carried with them a sense of joyous anticipation.

The year was barely underway when preparations for Carnevale were in order. This came just before the season of Lent, which meant a long period of fasting and, in those days, abstinence from meat. So, naturally, before the fasting came the feasting. Incidentally, Sicilians do not say Carnevale, but Carnilivari, which is derived from the phrase "carnem levare," to take away meat.

On the occasion of Carnilivari, the anticipated treat was homemade macaroni served with a special pork sauce, which invariably included little roll-ups made of pigskin enclosing a fragrant bread dressing. The macaroni for this dish was prepared from a pasta dough made with fewer eggs than our regular homemade noodles. Small portions of the dough were wrapped around the length of a reed-like stick that was lightly oiled until it was perfectly smooth. The trick was to deftly pull out the reed, leaving a long noodle with a hole through it. These were painstakingly made one at a time and hung to dry over a clean rod until it was time to drop them into boiling water. The taste of this macaroni, served with the rich meat sauce and distinctive pork roll-ups, was a taste treat to be cherished until the next Carnilivari.

On March 19, several weeks into the Lenten season, the Feast of Saint Joseph would come around. Because it was Lent, we ate no meat for this commemoration, but looked forward to the delicious specialties of the day, such as Pasta con le Sarde and other dishes using fish, vegetables and eggs. Another much-anticipated menu item was sfinge, sweet fritters made of yeast dough and drizzled with syrup, sugar and cinnamon. Although this was a simple private celebration for the Sodaros, some Sicilian families brought the elaborate custom of the Saint Joseph's Day table with them when they came to America. These tables were an act of devotion presented to the saint in thanksgiving for favors granted. If the family was not wealthy, the food was obtained through solicitation, and preparations often started weeks in advance.

The festivities always began with a Mass in honor of Saint Joseph, after which everyone retired to the home of the host. Three young children, representing the Holy Family, knocked at the door and were invited to enter. The parish priest blessed all the food, and the Holy Family were the first to be served. This hospitality prevailed throughout the day, and everyone who came to the door was made welcome and fed. The splendor of the table often exceeded any holiday meal, even Christmas or Easter. A table set with the finest linens held a statue of Saint Joseph in a place of honor and an array of foods that included fish, beans, salads, meatless pastas, omelets, and vegetables such as eggplant, stuffed artichokes and vegetable fritters. Breads, often baked in elaborate shapes, were given a place of importance, and the table was completed with a display of choicest fruits and dessert specialties.

Saint Joseph's Day was followed closely by Easter, but not before a flurry of housecleaning, floor polishing and curtain stretching during the week before Palm Sunday. Then came Holy Week devotions and, finally, the Easter baking. My mother would fashion biscotti dough into the shape of dolls and arrange a hard-cooked egg on each one before baking them. She then decorated the whole creation with confectioners' icing and sprinkled each generously with colored candies. She also used raisins to decorate the face with eyes, a nose and a mouth. These were called pupi cu'uova (dolls with eggs) and were presented to each of the girls in the family. For the boys, she rolled the dough into long, thick strips and braided them into a chain with an egg nestled in each twist. These were decorated the same as the pupi. A very small boy would have only one twist (with one egg) while older boys had two or three eggs. Papa, one of the "older boys," was always sure to get three eggs.

Summer brought its own diversions, with outdoor festivals sponsored by various religious societies. These always included processions through the streets with members of the society bearing a statue of Saint Rocco, or whichever saint was being honored. One of these feasts was held on Loomis Street between Polk and Taylor streets, directly in front of our house. I recall the carnival atmosphere that prevailed, with electric lights strung up and down the street, the merry-go-round hammering out its calliope music, the smell of Italian sausage roasting over hot coals, and vendors selling watermelon, Italian lemonade and assorted roasted beans such as ceci, semenza and lupini. On these special summer nights we were allowed to stay up late, sitting on our front steps with neighbors and friends, taking in the sights and scents of the festivities. It also gave us a special vantage point from which to enjoy the sounds of the local musicians performing on a platform built across from our house in front of Mazzuca's grocery store.

One of the most anticipated festivals of the summer was the Feast of the Assumption of the Blessed Mother, held on August 15. This celebration was held in very high regard in Termini Imerese, Sicily, where my parents and grandparents were born. In Sicily, the feast was preceded by nine days of devotional prayer known as a novena. On the eve of the feast, the devoted not only abstained from meat, but also from any animal products such as cheese, butter and eggs. I remember clearly that on August 14 the adults ate only boiled macaroni served with a little olive oil and some of the macaroni water.

My older cousin, Augusta Dugo, told me that, before I was born, the family lived in another location east of Racine Avenue, between Harrison and Polk streets. Family members lived in three buildings that shared a common courtyard, providing even more opportunities for togetherness. Augusta told me that, in those early days, our grandmother set up a statue of Our Lady in the courtyard and, for nine nights preceding the feast, family and friends would gather in the courtyard, light candles before the statue and hold novena devotions. On August 15, tables laden with food were set up in the courtyard and everyone came to eat and enjoy. While the women socialized, the men played a few games of cards and bocce and drank of their best wines, comparing and judging the quality of different barrels.

Each season brought its own activities, and early fall meant a flurry of canning and storing away for the winter months. I particularly remember the preparation of tomato paste, which was dried and cured in the sun on clean wooden frames that my grandfather made from orange and lemon crates. The tomato paste was spread out on boards and covered with clean white netting to keep flies away. Several times a day, the netting was removed and the paste stirred. In the evening, the boards were brought indoors. The process would be repeated for several days until the paste was sufficiently dry. It was then stored away for the winter in crockery jars with basil leaves nestled in each jar and a layer of olive oil covering the surface of the paste. This extract of tomato was called 'stratu. Those who enjoy dishes featuring sun-dried tomatoes, currently so popular in Italian restaurants, can appreciate the special flavor that made this long process worthwhile.

Later in the fall, the grapes would be delivered and the men would go about the business of making wine. The women would also get involved, however, preparing a sweet dessert wine from muscatel grapes that was especially delicious served ice cold over sliced fruits, or as an accompaniment to homemade biscotti.

Another concoction the ladies made with the grapes was vino cotto (cooked wine). This combination of grape juice and sugar was cooked very slowly until it became a syrup. It was used as a binding and sweetening agent for many special dishes, particularly in the fig and raisin cookies that were a Christmas specialty.

As Halloween approached, the children anticipated receiving treats, but not in the American tradition. The first day of November is All Saints' Day, followed immediately by All Souls' Day. I'm told that, in Sicily, children knew nothing of Babbo Natale or La Befana. Instead, on the night before All Souls' Day, they were reminded to recite prayers for the holy souls before going to bed and to hang a little shoe or small basket at the window. In the morning, the children would find small gifts from the holy souls, usually marzipan candies in various shapes, as well as oranges and nuts. I can remember only a few times when the marzipan candy made an appearance in our home, as the practice was somewhat lost here. It was kept alive more in the telling of it.

In Italy, the period of preparation for Christmas begins on December 13, the feast of Saint Lucy. Stalls are set up on the streets and in the piazzas to sell holiday items such as seasonal sweets and figurines for the elaborate Nativity scenes (presepii) that many families display. However, in most Sicilian homes, including ours, the Feast of Saint Lucy was a special observance, a day when bread disappeared from our table and in its place there appeared cuccia, panelle and special rice dishes. My mother, fearful that the children would cry for bread, would wrap whatever bread remained in the house in a large clean dish towel and carefully store it away in the bottom of our dining room china cabinet. In due time, we discovered the bread in its hiding place, but we never let on. We went along with the routine of the day, which was much more interesting.

On Saint Lucy's Day, the family abstained from any food that contained wheat flour, but there were still many special foods that were prepared to celebrate the occasion. One that I've already mentioned, panelle, is a pancake-like fritter that is prepared from ceci (chickpea) flour. It was seasoned with salt and parsley, boiled as for polenta, then poured on special wooden forms to cool and solidify. Finally, it was cut into small rectangles, deep fried in hot olive oil and served piping hot. In the morning, we would awaken to the smell of the panelle, and my mother would have a pot of cuccia cooking on the coal stove. Cuccia is the whole kernel of wheat grain, soaked overnight and prepared as a cereal. (Although food made from wheat flour is prohibited, unmilled wheat is eaten.) Incidentally, the bowls of the cuccia were sweetened with vino cotto, the cooked grape syrup previously described. The entire day continued in this manner, with panelle appearing in place of bread at every meal. Instead of the pasta we were accustomed to having for our evening meal, my mother would prepare Riso 'Ncasciato, a casserole of layered rice and vegetables.

As I grew older, I began to wonder why we ate only unmilled wheat products on the feast of Saint Lucy. I knew from my religious education that Saint Lucy was a virgin and martyr born in Siracusa, Sicily, who died for her virtue; but I only discovered her connection to wheat after many years of inquiry and reading. Legend has it that, at the time of her death, a terrible famine came to an end when ships laden with wheat miraculously appeared, then disappeared, after depositing huge quantities of the grain on the shore. The legend continues that the starving villagers did not wait for it to be milled into flour but boiled it and ate it as a pudding or cereal.

After December 13, preparations began in earnest for Christmas. Most of my memories of the weeks preceding Christmas center on the family's religious observance of the season and the special kitchen aromas that, for me, spelled love and foretold of family gatherings.

Christmas Eve, la Vigilia di Natale, would begin with my mother serving our family of seven a meal around our kitchen table. We upheld the Christmas Eve tradition in which no meat was eaten. Fish in many varieties appeared: baked, fried, in pasta sauces and more. Usually my mother served seven different types of fish, which she told us represented the seven sacraments. We would also eat salads and vegetables, roasted nuts, fruit and wine. After dinner, we joined all the aunts, uncles and cousins at Grandma's house. When I reminisced with my cousin Augusta about these long-ago Christmases this is how she remembered them:

"After dinner, the whole family would gather at Grandma's. We would play 7-1/2 for hazelnuts that we picked out of the holiday nut bowl. We also played lotto for a penny a card, and when we tired of that, there was another simple game called minigaddu. No one ever explained what it meant, but we began by having each player put one or two pennies in the kitty. Then a deck of cards was passed around the table face-up with each player exposing the next card. The game came to an abrupt end when the two of clubs appeared, and that player won the kitty. Towards midnight, Grandma and the aunts went into the kitchen to start preparing the midnight feast. They fried homemade sausage and made pizzas and mufuletti (homemade cheese buns). Just before midnight, Grandma would kneel before Uncle Tony's elaborate presepio and sing hymns of the Christ child. The whole family gathered around her and joined in the singing. When Uncle Gus was present, he would play the violin, which added a special touch to the spirit of the evening. After midnight, the ladies would put the food they had prepared on the table along with bowls of fruit, roasted chestnuts, and the special biscotti and cucciddati they had been baking for weeks. Shortly after this, the women and children would retire, but the men would play cards well into the night."

There were neither gifts nor a Santa Claus associated with these holiday gatherings. We were introduced to this idea at the parish church, where Santa would appear in the school hall with bags of candy, nuts and fruit for all the children.

Christmas Day meant morning Mass, followed by a fine meal of pasta and a special roast. Both the religious and secular celebrations extended until the Feast of the Epiphany on January 6. But most of my memories revolve around the rituals of Christmas Eve.

Like most people of my time and place, my early life centered on family, the church and the neighborhood. As personal as my ethnic experiences are to me, I know they are shared by anyone who has lived where urban gardens were planted; where the aroma of simmering spaghetti sauce filled one's nostrils as one walked home from Sunday Mass; where grape arbors flourished and wine presses were put to use in the fall; where grandmas and grandpas, aunts and uncles were always in view.

I continue the customs and food rituals of my childhood not only because they remind me of who I am, but also because, by some magic, certain days and certain dishes make the family of my childhood come to life in my mind's eye and I can almost feel their presence.

Antipasti
Appetizers

Antipasti Diversi	12
Peperoni Rossi Arrostiti	12
Olive Schiacciate	13
Fagioli Marinati	13
Frittata di Asparagi e Funghi	14
Zucchine alla Griglia	15
Melanzane con Salsa di Aceto e Aglio	16
Caponatina	17
Carciofi Fritti	18
Frittelle di Verdure	19
Gamberi Marinati	20
Frutti di Mare	21
Antipasto di Salsicce e Peperoni	22

Antipasti Diversi
Antipasto Tray

An antipasto tray may be arranged with some of the recipe suggestions in this chapter, such as Cracked Olive Salad, Roasted Red Peppers and any of the marinated fish or vegetables. In addition, you may add black olives, chunks of Italian cheese and slices of Italian luncheon meat as desired.

The important thing to remember is to arrange your tray attractively, using fresh green curly endive, parsley, radish roses and carrot curls to divide and decorate the arrangement. You may also wish to add a selection of hot items.

A variety of pizzas, either homemade or commercial, may be cut into small pieces (1-1/2- to 2-inches square) and served piping hot along with other tasty tidbits. This works particularly well when presenting a substantial party buffet.

The pizzas may be prepared in advance, cooled and cut into serving pieces and stored in a pan covered with aluminum foil. When ready to serve, place the pan in a preheated 375-degree oven for about 7 minutes, or until the pizza is piping hot.

Ann Explains…
The word "antipasto" is equivalent to the French "hors d'oeuvre" or the English "appetizer." It means "before the meal," and its presentation may be simple or elaborate.

Peperoni Rossi Arrostiti
Roasted Red Peppers

Select well-shaped peppers of uniform size. Wash, dry and place them under a broiler. Watch carefully and turn often until they are blistered and lightly charred on all sides.

Carefully place the peppers in a paper bag, close the bag and leave in the sink for about 15 minutes. The steam created will loosen the skins. Working with one pepper at a time, remove the skin under running water, setting the peppers in a colander until they are all peeled. Remove the stems, seeds and white membranes. A small knife will be helpful in scraping off any remaining skin or seeds.

Slice the peppers and toss with olive oil to coat, then add salt and pepper. Store in a covered container with slices of garlic to taste. Make 1 day ahead and serve as an antipasto or salad garnish.

Ann's Tips…
When shopping for olive oil, you will notice the availability of various types (and prices). I recommend keeping different grades on hand. Use a tasty but less expensive olive oil for sautéing and save your fruity virgin and extra virgin oils for salads and dishes like this one, in which the flavor of the oil can be fully appreciated.

Olive Schiacciate
Cracked Olive Salad

1 pound green Italian olives
1 large red or yellow onion, sliced
1 large clove garlic, cut in half
1/2 cup sliced celery
1/4 cup wine vinegar
1 tablespoon chopped fresh basil, or 1 teaspoon dried
1/2 teaspoon oregano
1/2 cup olive oil
Salt and pepper
A few red pepper flakes (optional)

Wash and drain the olives and dry on paper towels. Crack each olive with a mallet or the bottom of a heavy cup. Combine the olives with all the other ingredients and mix well. Keep in a covered jar in the refrigerator for at least 2 days. Use as a side dish or as part of an antipasto platter.

Ann's Tips...
This makes an excellent snack when served with crusty Italian bread.

Fagioli Marinati
Marinated Beans

2 (16-ounce) cans Great Northern beans
2 or 3 medium plum tomatoes
2 tablespoons sliced green onion, or 2 tablespoons chopped shallots
2 tablespoons chopped fresh parsley, or 1-1/2 teaspoons dried
Salad Dressing One (Page 24)

Drain the beans very well. Cut the tomatoes in half, scoop out and discard the seeds, then dice into small pieces. Toss with the beans and other ingredients, using enough dressing to moisten and flavor the beans. If Salad Dressing One is not used, use a dressing or marinade made with olive oil and flavored with garlic. Serve as part of an antipasto tray or as a salad in a lettuce-lined bowl.

Ann's Tips...
You might want to try this dish with chickpeas instead of Great Northern beans.

Frittata di Asparagi e Funghi
Asparagus and Mushroom Omelet

1 bunch asparagus
1/2 pound fresh mushrooms
1 medium onion
1/3 cup olive oil
1 clove garlic, whole
2 large fresh basil leaves, minced, or 1/2 teaspoon dried
1/2 teaspoon oregano
Salt and pepper to taste
6 eggs
1/3 cup grated Romano or Parmesan cheese
2 tablespoons minced fresh parsley
1/2 cup coarsely grated Fontinella or Swiss cheese

Ann's Tips...

This or any other savory vegetable frittata may be served as a warm appetizer. Cut it in wedges and offer your favorite bread as an accompaniment. It also makes a satisfying luncheon meal or light supper.

To prepare the asparagus, remove the scales, break off and discard the tough bottoms, and cut the asparagus into pieces. Wash and set aside. Wash the mushrooms quickly under lukewarm water, dry with paper towels, then slice and set aside. Thinly slice the onion and keep separate.

Fry each vegetable separately to ensure proper cooking. In a large, non-stick frying pan (10- or 12-inches wide), heat the oil and add the asparagus and garlic. Cook, stirring often, until the asparagus is lightly browned and tender. Remove to a dish with a slotted spoon and discard the garlic. Add the mushrooms to the pan and sauté over a medium-high heat until the moisture dries out and they are lightly browned. Remove with a slotted spoon and add to the asparagus. Now place the onions in the pan, adding more oil only if needed, and cook over a low heat until they are soft and golden. Add the reserved asparagus and mushrooms to the pan and season with basil, oregano, salt and pepper.

Beat the eggs in a medium-sized bowl, adding Romano or Parmesan cheese, parsley and a little salt. Pour over the vegetables in the frying pan and cook over a medium heat. Lift the egg around the edges as it sets, allowing the uncooked egg to slip under. When there is no more loose egg on top of the omelet, cover it with Fontinella or Swiss cheese and place it in a preheated broiler to set the top and melt the cheese. Slip it onto a large round platter and serve at once.

Zucchine alla Griglia
Grilled Zucchini

4 to 6 medium zucchini
2 to 3 tablespoons olive oil
Garlic salt
Grated Romano or Parmesan cheese
Fresh basil or mint leaves, minced

Lightly scrape, rinse and dry the zucchini. With a sharp knife, cut in diagonal slices 1/3-inch thick. Lightly brush each slice on both sides with olive oil and set aside.

Make a medium-hot fire with either a charcoal or gas grill. Coat the grill rack with a non-stick spray before starting the fire. Place the zucchini slices on the hot grill, fairly close together. If the grill has a cover, close it, then check after 4 to 5 minutes, turning the slices when golden brown. Repeat with the second side, continuing until all are cooked.

Arrange the cooked zucchini in a layer on a serving dish and sprinkle lightly with garlic salt, cheese and basil or mint. Cover with a second layer and repeat the seasonings. Continue layering until all are seasoned.

Cook's Note: As a variation, the layers may be seasoned with garlic-flavored wine vinegar, oregano, basil, parsley, thinly sliced green onions, salt and pepper.

Ann Explains...

Grilled vegetables are showing up on many restaurant menus today as part of an antipasto, as a side dish or even in vegetarian sandwiches. This method of grilling is also suitable for other vegetables, especially small eggplants.

Melanzane con Salsa di Aceto e Aglio
Eggplant with Garlic and Vinegar Sauce

1 large eggplant
Olive oil
2 cloves garlic
1/3 cup wine vinegar
Oregano
Basil
Salt and pepper
Red pepper flakes

Ann's Tips...

*Sprinkling the eggplant
with salt, layering it between
sheets of paper towel and
setting a heavy object on top
for a half an hour releases
some of the juices from the
eggplant and makes
it less bitter.*

Peel and wash the eggplant, then cut into halves crosswise. Cut each half into lengthwise slices about 1/4-inch thick. (If you wish, they may then be cut into finger-size widths.) Sprinkle the slices with salt and place on a plate in layers between sheets of paper towel. Put a heavy bowl or something else of weight on top and allow to rest for 1/2 hour. Pat dry with paper towels.

Heat at least 1/2 cup of oil until it is very hot. Brown as many slices at a time as you can without crowding the pan. If using strips, put only enough to make one layer. Watch carefully and, when they are golden brown, remove to a plate with a slotted spoon. Proceed until all the eggplant is cooked. Cut the garlic into slivers and sauté lightly in remaining oil. If necessary, add more oil. Add vinegar and cook about 5 minutes.

Layer the eggplant in a flat-bottomed bowl, adding oregano, basil, red pepper flakes, salt and pepper to taste. Continue with another layer in the same manner. Pour the hot oil-vinegar mixture over the eggplant. Cool and serve.

Antipasti ❦ Appetizers

Caponatina
Eggplant and Tomato Appetizer

4 medium eggplants

4 ribs celery, finely diced

1-1/2 cups olive oil

4 onions, sliced

1-1/2 cups tomato sauce

1/4 cup capers, rinsed and drained

2 tablespoons pine nuts

12 green olives, pitted and cut into pieces

1/2 cup wine vinegar

1/4 cup sugar

1 teaspoon salt

1/2 teaspoon pepper

Peel the eggplants and cut into 1-inch pieces. Sprinkle the pieces with salt and place on a plate in layers between sheets of paper towel. Put a heavy bowl or something else of weight on top and allow to rest for 1/2 hour. Afterward, pat dry with paper towels. Parboil the celery in a small amount of water for 2 minutes. Drain and set aside.

Heat 1 cup of oil in a frying pan and add the eggplant after squeezing it dry of moisture. Sauté until golden brown and remove to a dish with a slotted spoon. Add another 1/2 cup of oil to the pan. Heat and sauté the onions until they are soft but not browned. Add the parboiled celery and tomato sauce. Simmer the mixture for 15 minutes, stirring often. Add the capers, pine nuts and olives.

In a small saucepan, heat the wine vinegar and dissolve the sugar and salt in it. Add this and the sautéed eggplant to the sauce. Add the pepper and stir the mixture well. Cover and simmer over a low heat for 20 minutes, stirring often.

Ann's Tips...
Caponatina can be served at room temperature. Be sure to have a basket of freshly sliced French bread close at hand.

Carciofi Fritti
Breaded Artichoke Hearts

4 to 6 medium artichokes
2 cups bread crumbs
1 clove garlic, crushed or minced
1 tablespoon grated Romano or Parmesan cheese
1 tablespoon or more coarsely chopped fresh parsley
Salt and pepper to taste
2 eggs

Peel off all the leaves from each artichoke, and scoop out the fuzzy "choke" with a spoon. Cut each heart into 4 to 6 slices and set aside. Add the bread crumbs to the garlic, cheese, parsley, salt and pepper, then mix well. Beat the eggs. Dip the artichoke slices in the eggs and pass them through the bread crumbs. Let them stand for 20 minutes, then fry in deep oil.

Ann Explains...
This recipe is from good cook and good friend Tena Amico. Serve as a savory appetizer or as a side dish.

Frittelle di Verdure
Batter-Fried Vegetables

Cauliflower florets, partially cooked
Broccoli florets, partially cooked
1 cup flour
1/2 teaspoon salt
Pepper to taste
3/4 cup milk
1 large egg
1 tablespoon melted butter
Garlic powder (optional)
Onion powder (optional)
Grated Romano or Parmesan cheese (optional)

Prepare the vegetables and set aside. Combine the flour, salt and pepper, and set aside. Beat together the milk, egg and butter. Gradually sprinkle in the flour mixture, beating until smooth. Add garlic and onion powders if desired.

Fill a deep saucepan 1/2- to 2/3-full with cooking oil and heat thoroughly over a medium-high flame. Dip vegetable pieces in the batter and fry in hot oil, being careful not to crowd the pieces. Fry about 5 minutes or until golden brown, turning occasionally. Remove with a slotted spoon, draining off excess oil. Place on paper towels while frying any remaining vegetables. Place on a warm platter, sprinkle with grated cheese if desired, and serve immediately.

Ann's Tips...
Cauliflower and broccoli florets are listed as the main ingredients here, but any of a variety of vegetables can be used, including zucchini (sliced and raw), cardoons (cooked and sliced, when available) and sliced artichoke hearts (or canned artichoke hearts, well drained).

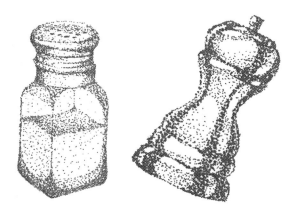

Gamberi Marinati
Marinated Shrimp

Ann's Tips...
This dish may be
served as part of an
antipasto platter or on
individual plates,
lined with leaf lettuce
and garnished with
ripe olives and slices
of hard-boiled eggs.

1-1/2 pounds shrimp
1 teaspoon dehydrated minced onion
1/8 teaspoon red pepper flakes
2 or 3 green onions, sliced
1/4 medium green or red pepper, diced (optional)
2 tablespoons chopped fresh parsley, or 1 teaspoon dried
2 ribs celery heart, thinly sliced
Salad Dressing Two or Three (Pages 24-25)

Rinse the shrimp and cook in salted water to cover, together with the dehydrated onion and red pepper flakes. Simmer, covered, for 2 to 5 minutes, or until pink. Do not overcook. Drain, cool and clean the shrimp, removing the shells and back veins. Toss with the other ingredients, adding salad dressing to taste. Chill in the refrigerator.

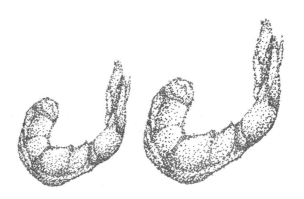

Frutti di Mare
Seafood Salad

1 pound medium shrimp
1 pound calamari, cleaned and cut into rings
1/2 pound bay scallops or sea scallops
1 small onion, diced
1/2 cup minced celery
2 tablespoons minced red or green pepper (optional)
Condimento di Limone ed Olio (Page 26)
Parsley for garnish (optional)

Cook the shrimp, calamari and scallops separately in boiling salted water with 1 tablespoon of lemon juice added.

Cook the shrimp 2 to 5 minutes or until they turn pink. Remove the shells and back veins.

To cook the calamari, add them to boiling water, reduce to a simmer, and cook approximately 10 to 15 minutes. Test for doneness. The rings should not be rubbery.

If sea scallops are used cut them each in half. Cook the scallops only until they are no longer translucent. After about 1 minute they will appear white and they are done.

Combine the prepared seafood with the remaining ingredients and mix well. Chill. At serving time place in a bowl using a slotted spoon. Pour some of the Lemon Dressing over the seafood. Sprinkle with snips of parsley if desired.

Cook's Note: See Page 86 for tips on cleaning calamari.

Menu Suggestion

Christmas Eve Dinner

Mufuletti

•

Spaghetti con Salsa di Calamari

•

Muddica

•

Pesce Spada Fritto

•

Frutti di Mare

•

Baccalà alla Siciliana

•

Broccoli con Salsa di Limone

•

Peperoni Rossi Arrostiti

•

Finocchi

•

Pesche al Vino

•

Assortimento di Biscotti

•

Antipasto di Salsicce e Peperoni
Sausage and Pepper Appetizer

6 links Italian sausage
3 green or red peppers
1 clove garlic, cut in half
Salt and pepper to taste
Dash each: basil, oregano, onion powder

Prepare sausage links by frying or oven baking them. If desired, home-made sausage mixture (Page 114) may be shaped into miniature meat-balls and baked on a cookie sheet, then set aside.

Wash and cut green peppers into 1-1/2-inch squares. Pat dry and add to a frying pan with enough hot oil to cover the bottom. Cook over a medium heat, stirring often, to prevent scorching. When half done, add the garlic and season with salt and pepper. Sprinkle lightly with basil, oregano and onion powder. Cover and continue cooking until tender but not too soft. Discard the garlic.

Cut the cooked sausage into slices less than 1-inch thick. Put togeth-er a piece of sausage on top of a pepper square, spear with a frilled wooden pick, and arrange on a tray. Serve hot. To prepare in advance, arrange the sausage and peppers on cookie sheets. At serving time, place in a preheated 375-degree oven until hot. Secure with frilled wooden picks and serve.

Ann's Tips...

At most Italian tables there are no set rules governing which foods are served as openers. In other chapters of this book, you will find recipes such as Arancini, Calzone or Bruschetta that are often served as a snack or an antipasto course. Use your imagination to expand your choices.

Antipasti ❀ Appetizers

Insalate
Salads

Italian Salad Dressing One

1/3 cup wine vinegar
1/2 teaspoon salt, or to taste
1/2 teaspoon onion salt
1 clove garlic, cut in half, or 1/2 teaspoon garlic powder
1/2 teaspoon each: oregano, basil
Pepper (optional)
1 cup olive oil

Ann's Tips...
When substituting dried herbs for fresh herbs, a good rule of thumb is to use 1/3 to 1/2 teaspoon of dried herbs for every tablespoon of fresh.

Stir all of the seasonings into the vinegar and mix well in a cruet. Add the oil, mix well and taste to correct seasonings. Shake well each time before using. Store in the refrigerator.

Italian Salad Dressing Two

1/2 cup tarragon or wine vinegar
1 teaspoon salt
1 teaspoon mustard
1 teaspoon paprika
1/2 teaspoon pepper
1 cup olive oil

Mix all the ingredients in a tightly covered jar. Store in the refrigerator. This dressing is good on bean salads, etc. Part lemon juice may be substituted for vinegar.

Italian Salad Dressing Three

1 recipe Salad Dressing Two (Page 24), reduce salt if desired
1 hard-boiled egg yolk, mashed
3 anchovy fillets, mashed
1 small clove garlic, through a press
1/2 teaspoon dried parsley flakes
1/2 teaspoon thyme
Paprika (optional)

Have ready all the ingredients from Salad Dressing Two but proceed as directed below. Mash hard-boiled egg yolk or put through a sieve. Cut each anchovy in small pieces, then work into the yolk, mashing as you mix. Add the garlic, parsley, thyme, salt, mustard, optional paprika and pepper. At this point, the above ingredients may be put into a blender with the vinegar to mix. Gradually add the oil and blend until the dressing is completely mixed. If you prefer, the ingredients may be mixed by shaking very well in a tightly covered jar or by beating vigorously with a wire whisk. Store in the refrigerator. This dressing mimics the flavor of a Caesar salad while avoiding the risks associated today with serving raw eggs. Try this one with torn romaine lettuce, homemade croutons and, if desired, a grating of fresh Romano cheese.

Italian Proverb

"Un piatto di lattuga, l'insonnia mette in fuga."

•

(A plate of lettuce keeps insomnia away.)

•

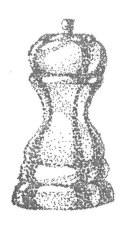

Condimento di Limone ed Olio
Lemon and Oil Dressing

1/2 cup lemon juice from fresh lemons
1 clove garlic, through a press
1 tablespoon chopped fresh parsley, or 1 teaspoon dried
3 large basil leaves, chopped, or 1 teaspoon dried
2 fresh mint leaves, chopped, or 1/2 teaspoon dried
1/2 teaspoon oregano, or to taste
1/2 teaspoon onion salt
1/2 teaspoon salt, or to taste
1/2 teaspoon Worcestershire sauce
1/4 teaspoon freshly ground pepper, or more, to taste
1 cup olive oil

Ream the juice from 2 or 3 lemons, until 1/2 cup is accumulated. Put it in a bowl and add all the ingredients except the oil. Mix and stir to dissolve the salts. Add the oil, slowly beating it into the juice mixture. If it is not used immediately, store the dressing in a tightly covered jar in the refrigerator. Shake well before each use.

Ann's Tips...

Lemons are a truly versatile fruit, enhancing the flavor of soups, fish and desserts alike. In our family, we also use them with meat and poultry dishes and, of course, salads. This lemon and oil dressing works well with many dishes.

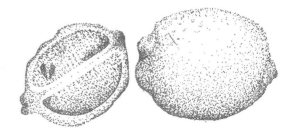

Insalata di Verdura Italiana
Green Italian Salad

When making a green salad, select vegetables that are of the highest quality and at the peak of their perfection. Wash greens such as lettuce, endive, escarole, celery, carrots, parsley, etc. Shake them free of excess water and leave them in a colander to rest awhile. Pat as dry as possible, then store in plastic bags or containers, using the vegetable drawer of your refrigerator when available. It is best to prepare these vegetables at least a day in advance, as it helps to crisp the greens.

On the day that the salad is to be made, the variety and amount of greens you need can be torn into a bowl, covered and stored in the refrigerator again. Just before serving, add sliced tomatoes and toss with dressing. Seasoned croutons may be added at this time.

To make an antipasto salad, add strips of salami, provolone or mortadella, along with anchovies, olives and hard-boiled egg wedges. This makes an excellent luncheon salad, but can also be served when you wish to omit a separate antipasto course at a dinner party.

Insalata di Arance alla Siciliana
Sicilian Orange Salad

3 or 4 seedless oranges
3/4 cup pitted ripe olives
4 ounces Gorgonzola cheese, crumbled
Red or white sweet onion, cut into rings
Salt and pepper
2 tablespoons olive oil, or more, to taste

Peel the oranges carefully, removing as much white part as possible. With a sharp, serrated knife, cut the oranges into slices (not wedges). Collect any juice that accumulates in slicing and reserve. Pile olives in the center of a platter that may or may not be lined with lettuce. Arrange the orange slices in an overlapping pattern, filling the platter. Crumble Gorgonzola cheese and distribute it over the orange slices along with the onion rings. Season with the salt and pepper. Mix olive oil with the reserved orange juice and pour it over the oranges. Serve with fresh crusty bread.

Ann's Tips...

Homemade croutons are a nice touch and a good way to make use of Italian bread that is starting to get dry. Trim the crust from the bread and cut it into cubes. Place in a baking pan or on a cookie sheet and drizzle with olive oil. If desired, sprinkle with grated Parmesan cheese or a favorite herb or spice. Toss to coat the cubes and bake in a preheated 325-degree oven until golden. Watch carefully and stir occasionally.

Ann Remembers...

When I was a girl, my mother would occasionally serve sliced oranges dressed as a salad. At the time, I thought this quite strange. It wasn't until much later that I learned that orange salad is quite popular in Sicily, where lemons and oranges grow in abundance. Today, it is often featured in restaurants and magazines as California or Sunburst Salad.

Insalata di Pomodoro
Tomato Salad

3 or 4 large ripe firm tomatoes, sliced
Leaf lettuce
Provolone or Fontinella cheese, cubed
Cured black Italian olives, or canned ripe
Red or white sweet onion, thinly sliced
2 or 3 tablespoons capers, rinsed and dried
Fresh basil, minced
Salt and pepper
Olive oil
Vinegar (optional)

Ann's Tips...
In our family, we enjoy tomatoes fresh from the garden with a generous drizzle of olive oil, but without vinegar. You may add it if you prefer.

Wash the tomatoes and lettuce and pat dry. Line a round or oblong platter with lettuce leaves. Pile the cheese in the center of the platter. Surround the cheese with olives. Arrange the tomatoes in an overlapping pattern around the outside edge of the platter. Over the tomatoes arrange onion rings, capers, basil, salt and pepper. Drizzle olive oil over them. If desired, vinegar may also be used.

Insalata Caprese
Tomato and Mozzarella Salad

3 or 4 firm ripe tomatoes, sliced
Leaf lettuce (optional)
Fresh mozzarella cheese, sliced
Red or white sweet onion rings (optional)
Fresh basil, chopped
Oregano
Salt and pepper
Olive oil
Vinegar (optional)

Ann's Tips...
Of all the pleasures available to the home gardener, none can surpass the delight of the first bite of a vine-ripened tomato. Just thinking about a platter of red, sliced tomatoes nestled together with fresh mozzarella, thinly sliced garden onion and minced fresh basil is enough to make your taste buds come alive.

Arrange sliced tomatoes in an overlapping pattern on a lettuce-lined dish. Tuck slices of fresh mozzarella cheese between each slice of tomato. Cover with onion rings and basil, and sprinkle some oregano over all. Season with salt and pepper and drizzle with olive oil. Vinegar may be used if desired, and onion rings may be omitted.

Insalata di Pollo
Grilled Chicken Salad

6 to 8 large chicken breasts, skinned and boned
3 tablespoons olive oil
2 tablespoons melted butter or margarine
1 large clove garlic, through a press
1/2 teaspoon onion salt, or to taste
1/8 teaspoon pepper
1/2 teaspoon each: oregano, basil
1 teaspoon dried parsley flakes (fresh herbs may be used when available)
1 teaspoon Worcestershire sauce
1/2 teaspoon A-1 sauce
1 recipe Condimento di Limone ed Olio (Page 26)
Paprika (optional)
Endive or other greens, washed and dried
Plum tomatoes, cut up (optional)
Small bunch fresh basil

Remove any fat from the chicken breasts, rinse and pat dry with paper towels. Combine olive oil with the next several ingredients, through the A-1 sauce. Dip each chicken breast in this mixture, then turn to coat the second side. Arrange them in a single layer on a non-aluminum platter or baking dish. Cover with plastic and refrigerate for 2 hours or overnight. Prepare the dressing and refrigerate until needed.

Make a medium-hot fire with either a charcoal or gas grill. Coat the grill rack with a non-stick spray before starting the fire. Place the chicken breasts on the grill, top side first, and cook for 7 minutes or until brown. Turn them to cook on the second side, about 5 minutes, or until the chicken is no longer pink in the center. Sprinkle lightly with paprika if desired, remove from grill and, when sufficiently cool, pack away in a covered dish and refrigerate for the next day.

On the picnic day, slice all the chicken breasts on a diagonal for thin, long slices. Pack again and put into a cooler until needed. Just before serving, cover a platter with the tender leaves of curly endive or other greens. Arrange the sliced chicken in an attractive pattern over them. Add plum tomatoes if desired. Shake the dressing and spoon over the chicken. Tear fresh basil leaves over the chicken and serve. This dish may be served hot off the grill if you wish.

Ann's Tips...

A family picnic should be a day for all to enjoy — even the cook. It helps to have recipes that can be prepared the day before the outing, such as this cold grilled chicken dish. Be sure everything is refrigerated and packed in a cooler when leaving for your picnic. And remember to include a good Italian bread, packed separately to keep it crisp.

Insalata di Riso
Rice Salad

2 cups rice
2 teaspoons Dijon mustard
1 teaspoon salt
4 teaspoons red wine vinegar
3/4 cup olive oil
1 cup finely diced Swiss cheese
1/2 cup sliced ripe olives
1/4 cup sliced green olives
1/2 cup diced sweet green and red pepper
2 whole chicken breasts, boiled and diced

Ann's Tips...
This is a very popular dish in Italy. You may substitute crab meat, lobster or tuna for the chicken, but if you do, I recommend that you omit the cheese.

Measure and wash the rice, place it in a pot with 1-1/2 quarts salted water and bring it to a boil. Reduce to a simmer and after stirring once, cover and cook until just tender. Drain, rinse in cold water and drain well again. Put the mustard, salt and vinegar in a large bowl and mix. Slowly add the oil, beating it into the vinegar mixture. Add the rice and toss to coat. Add the other ingredients and toss again. Serve at room temperature as a luncheon salad or as an antipasto.

Insalate ❀ Salads

Insalata di Cavolfiore alla Siciliana
Sicilian Cauliflower Salad

1 medium to large cauliflower
1-1/2 lemons
1/2 cup olive oil
1 tablespoon chopped fresh parsley
3 large basil leaves
1 clove garlic, through a press
1 tablespoon capers
1/4 teaspoon onion salt
1/4 teaspoon table salt, or to taste
8 large ripe olives
2 fresh mint leaves
3 green onions
2 ribs celery heart
6 anchovy fillets, halved
1 (6-1/2 ounce) can tuna, packed in water or olive oil
Pepper, freshly ground
Paprika

Prepare the cauliflower by cutting it into florets. Remove any tough or yellowed portion and include all tender green leaves. Cook it in 3 cups of boiling water with 1/2 teaspoon salt, covered, for 8 to 10 minutes, or until just tender. Do not overcook. Drain and let cool.

To prepare the dressing, ream the juice from the lemons and add the next 7 ingredients, reserving 2 basil leaves. Mix well and set aside. To prepare the garnish, cut the olives in fourths. Chop the mint leaves with the remaining basil leaves. Slice the green onions, including some green portion. Slice the celery thinly and halve the anchovy fillets. Set all aside.

To assemble, select a round or oblong platter and start arranging the cauliflower from the outside rim of the platter with the florets facing out. Continue arranging the florets in overlapping rows. Leave a 4-inch or 5-inch circle in the center. Place a well-drained can of tuna in the circle. (If the oil-packed tuna is used, include the oil.)

Arrange the prepared garnishes over all. Mix the dressing well and spoon over all. Sprinkle with pepper and paprika and serve with crusty Italian bread.

Ann's Tips...

Summer is a time for one-dish meals, creating less work for the cook and leaving more time for leisure. This cauliflower salad makes a good light supper or luncheon meal any time of the year.

Insalata di Fagiolini e Patate
Green Bean and Potato Salad

1 pound small new potatoes
3/4 pound young green beans
Cheese Dressing (recipe follows)
1 small red onion, sliced into rings
2 cups bite-sized pieces escarole (optional)
Grated Parmesan cheese

Italian Proverb

"La patata dà più forza, se
è cotta con la scorza."

•

(The potato gives more
strength if it is cooked
with the skin.)

•

Boil the potatoes in water for about 25 minutes, or until tender. Drain, cool, peel (if desired) and cut into cubes. Meanwhile, cook the string beans in lightly salted boiling water until just tender. Drain, run cold water over them to stop the cooking process and set aside. Prepare the Cheese Dressing.

In a large bowl, combine the potatoes, string beans, onion rings and Cheese Dressing. Toss lightly, coating all the vegetables well. Refrigerate covered for at least 2 hours. Just before serving, combine with the escarole if desired, and generously sprinkle with grated cheese.

Cheese Dressing

3/4 cup olive oil
1/4 cup red wine vinegar
2 tablespoons grated Parmesan cheese
1/2 teaspoon salt, or less, to taste
Pepper, freshly ground, to taste
1/2 teaspoon dried oregano

Combine all the dressing ingredients in a jar with a tight fitting lid, and shake well to mix.

Insalata di Fagiolini e Carciofi
Green Bean and Artichoke Salad

1-1/2 pounds fresh whole green beans
1 (10-ounce) package frozen artichoke hearts, thawed,
    or 1 large can artichoke hearts, drained
Red roasted peppers, homemade or commercial pack
Leaf lettuce
1 small red onion, quartered and thinly sliced,
    or 2 or 3 green onions, thinly sliced
2 tablespoons chopped fresh parsley
1/2 teaspoon basil
1/2 teaspoon oregano
1/2 teaspoon garlic salt, or to taste
Pepper, freshly ground
Tomatoes (optional)
1/2 cup Salad Dressing One (Page 24)

Wash the beans, break off the tips and cook in lightly-salted boiling water, covered, for about 15 minutes, or until tender. Cut the artichoke hearts in halves or fourths. Drain the roasted peppers and cut into thin strips.

This dish can be arranged on individual salad plates if desired. To serve family style, cover a platter with leaf lettuce. Arrange the green beans along the center of the platter with all the beans going in the same direction. Place the artichoke hearts on either side of the beans. Arrange the onion slices and pepper strips over the green beans and artichokes, and sprinkle all the seasonings across the top. The addition of tomato wedges enhances the flavor.

This salad may be prepared well in advance, covered with plastic wrap and refrigerated for several hours or overnight. Add salad dressing about an hour before serving.

Ann's Tips...

The food you serve your family and guests should look as good as it tastes. Take a few minutes to use garnishes or other finishing touches. Fresh greens lining the serving plate of cold foods, a sprinkling of paprika on vegetables that otherwise lack color, a bunch of parsley on a platter of meat, a sprig of holly on a holiday tray — these small things take only a moment and enhance the senses of those around your table.

Insalata di Tonno
Tuna Salad

1 cup tuna in oil
1/2 cup sliced celery
2 green onions, sliced
1 tablespoon chopped fresh parsley
Condimento di Limone ed Olio (Page 26)
   or juice of 1 lemon and 2 tablespoons olive oil
Salt and pepper to taste
Ripe olives, 2 hard-boiled eggs for garnish

Flake the tuna, add the next 3 ingredients with sufficient dressing to moisten. Substitute plain lemon juice and oil if desired. Season with salt and pepper. Serve on individual salad dishes lined with lettuce and garnished with ripe olives and quartered hard-boiled eggs.

Ann's Tips...

Before cutting lemons, roll them on a counter top or cutting board, pressing down with the palm of your hand. This allows you to extract the maximum amount of juice.

Insalata di Carne
Boiled Beef Salad

Boiled soup meat, removed from bone
2 or 3 green onions, sliced
2 tablespoons chopped fresh parsley
2 ribs celery, sliced
Salt and pepper
1 teaspoon capers (optional)
Tomato wedges, hard-boiled eggs, black olives for garnish (optional)
Dressing of choice

Trim off any fat from beef. Dice or shred the beef and put it into a bowl. Add green onions, parsley, celery, salt and pepper, and optional capers. Toss with a sufficient amount of dressing to wet the meat. Serve as is, with crusty bread, or on a lettuce-lined platter garnished with tomato wedges, hard-boiled egg wedges and black olives.

Ann Remembers...

When my mother made soup with meaty beef bones, she would save the choicest of the meat from the bones to make this delicious salad as an accompaniment to our meal. I suggest using Italian Salad Dressing One (Page 24) or Condimento di Limone ed Olio (Page 26) to create the ultimate "soup and salad" supper.

Zuppe e Minestre
Soups and Broths

Brodo di Manzo
Beef Broth

2 pounds beef with bone (blade or shinbone)
Additional soup bone (beef or veal knuckle) (optional)
2 quarts water
1 large onion, studded with 3 cloves
1 small potato
2 tomatoes, or 1 cup canned tomatoes
3 sprigs fresh parsley
2 large carrots
4 large celery ribs with leaves
1 small yellow turnip (optional)
1 tablespoon salt
1/4 teaspoon pepper, or 3 peppercorns
2 beef bouillon cubes

Ann Remembers...

In our home, my mother never made soup in which everything just went into the pot. For a more flavorful broth, she liked to make what she called a double-stock soup. First she made a basic stock, drained it, cooled it, then skimmed it of its fat. Only then was she ready to "make soup" by enhancing her broth with vegetables, pastina or whatever else pleased the cook.

Trim the meat of any excess fat and wipe clean or rinse under cold running water. Put the meat and optional soup bone into a large pot that has a lid, together with water to cover, and bring to a boil. After 10 minutes, skim off any foam that rises to the top of water.

Add all the vegetables and seasonings. (The turnip gives additional flavor, but is not essential.) When the water boils again, lower the heat to a simmer. Cover the pot and simmer for 2 hours, or until meat is tender. Remove the meat to a dish to cool.

Strain the soup through several layers of cheese cloth. Taste to correct the seasoning. The soup is now ready to use as a broth or as a base for heartier soups.

Cook's Note: Some or all of the beef removed from the broth may be used to prepare Insalata di Carne (Page 34).

Verdure in Brodo di Manzo
Vegetable Beef Soup

1 medium potato, diced
1 medium carrot, diced
1/2 cup sliced celery with leaves
1 small onion, diced
Large sprig fresh parsley, chopped
1 small turnip, sliced (optional)
1/2 cup peas, or sliced string beans
6 to 8 cups beef broth
Romano or Parmesan cheese, grated

Ann's Tips...
Many Sicilian cooks add tiny meatballs to their soups. For the method of preparation, see Brodo di Pollo con Pastina e Polpettine (Page 39).

Pare the potato and carrot and put them in a colander together with the other vegetables. Wash and drain. Bring the broth to a boil, add the vegetables, and cook until tender. If desired, a small amount of cooked pastina or rice may be added together with miniature meatballs. Pass the grated cheese.

From Ann's Kitchen

Brodo di Pollo
Chicken Broth

1 large chicken, 3-1/2 pounds or more,
  or 4- to 5-pound stewing chicken
Water to cover
1 large onion
1 small potato
3 large sprigs fresh parsley
2 carrots
4 large celery ribs with leaves
1 large tomato, or 1/2 cup canned tomatoes
1 tablespoon salt
1/2 teaspoon pepper, or 3 peppercorns
2 chicken bouillon cubes (optional)

Ann's Tips...

Although many cooks insist that a stewing chicken is essential for making good soups or broth, it is possible to attain excellent results with a large fryer or roasting chicken weighing 3-1/2 pounds or more. You can also use wings, necks, backs or other parts that are a good value at the market.

Clean and wash the chicken and put it into a large soup pot with water. Allow to come to a boil. After cooking 10 minutes over a medium heat, remove any foam that may form on top of the water. Add all the vegetables and seasonings. Return to a boil, turn down the heat to a simmer, cover the pot and cook 2- to 2-1/2 hours. If a stewing chicken is used, a longer cooking time may be necessary.

Remove the chicken and reserve for another use. Strain the soup through several layers of cheese cloth. If clear broth is desired, leave as is. For richer flavor, press the vegetables through a strainer and add to the soup pot. Prepare with homemade or commercial egg noodles for chicken noodle soup. If desired, some chicken may be boned and added to the soup, either by itself or with a few miniature meatballs and sliced vegetables.

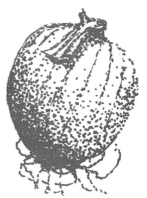

Brodo di Pollo con Pastina e Polpettine
Chicken Broth with Pastina and Tiny Meatballs

2 quarts chicken broth
1 cup pastina, cooked separately
Polpettine (recipe follows)
Romano or Parmesan cheese, grated

Drop Polpettine into boiling chicken broth. Simmer for about 30 minutes, then add the pastina. Heat and serve with grated cheese.

Polpettine

1/3 cup dry bread crumbs, or 1 cup soft
1/4 cup grated Romano cheese
2 teaspoons chopped fresh parsley
1 clove garlic, through a press or minced
1 teaspoon salt
1/8 teaspoon pepper
Dash nutmeg (optional)
1/3 cup water
2 small eggs
1 pound ground round or sirloin steak

Combine the crumbs, cheese and all the seasonings. Add the water to moisten the crumbs. Mix in the eggs, then add the ground meat in 2 or 3 portions, blending lightly but thoroughly. Form into tiny balls the size of marbles.

Cook's Note: If you prefer, you may precook the meatballs before adding them to the soup. This may be done in a skillet or in a pre-heated 350-degree oven. Either way, add approximately one tablespoon of olive oil to the pan and turn the meatballs occasionally until brown on all sides.

Ann Remembers...

Many of our food memories revolve around holiday feasts and the fancy foods served at large gatherings. But we also remember the simpler meals, relaxing meals served in the warmth of our mother's kitchen.

Minestrina di Cubetti
Chicken Soup with Cheese Cubes

Ann's Tips...

For this interesting soup, the seasoned ricotta cheese is prepared as for baked custard. The water that surrounds the baking dish should be about 2 inches deep. The correct firmness is achieved when the tip of an inserted knife comes out completely clean. If you wish, add minced parsley to the clear chicken broth for additional flavor and color.

10 ounces ricotta cheese, very well drained
1 egg plus 1 egg yolk
Nutmeg
2/3 cup grated Parmesan cheese
2 quarts clear chicken broth

Put the ricotta in a bowl and work thoroughly with a wooden spoon or spatula, beating it until it is quite smooth. An electric mixer also may be used. Add the egg and yolk, a good grating of nutmeg and the Parmesan cheese. When the mixture is well blended, spread it evenly in an 8-inch square buttered glass baking dish. Place the dish in a pan of hot water and bake it in a preheated 300-degree oven for 50 to 60 minutes, or until it is firm. Allow to cool. When ready to use, cut into 1/2-inch cubes, place in a soup tureen and pour boiling chicken broth over them. Serve hot.

Verdure in Brodo
Broth with Greens

Ann's Tips...

Any small pasta may be used in this soup, such as ditalini, tubetti, small shells, or even elbow macaroni.

3 tablespoons minced onion
Olive oil or butter
1/2 cup small pasta
1 large or 2 small heads escarole, or flat-leaf endive
6 to 8 cups hot strained chicken or beef broth
Dash each: nutmeg, thyme
Pepper (optional)
Romano or Parmesan cheese, grated

Sauté the onion in a small amount of oil or butter. Set aside. Cook the pasta in salted water, drain and set aside. Select fresh greens and separate the outer leaves, discarding any that are bruised or brown. Cut into pieces. Cut the heart of the endive or escarole into wedges. Wash thoroughly and cook in a small amount of salted boiling water until just tender. Drain well and add to the hot broth along with the onions, pasta and seasonings. Heat through and serve very hot together with crusty bread. Pass the grated cheese.

Minestra di Patate con lo Zafferano
Potato Soup with Saffron

4 medium red potatoes
1/4 cup olive oil
1 large clove garlic, minced
1 small piece hard Italian cheese (optional)
2 tablespoons chopped fresh parsley
4 cups water
1 teaspoon salt, or to taste
1/4 teaspoon pepper
1/8 teaspoon saffron

Pare the potatoes, cut them into a small dice, rinse and set aside. Heat the oil in a saucepan and add the garlic and optional cheese. Stir while cooking for about 1 minute, being careful not to burn the garlic. Add the potatoes and parsley and continue cooking, stirring for about 2 minutes, or until the potatoes are coated.

Add the water and seasonings and bring to a boil. Reduce to a simmer, cover and cook for 20 minutes. Remove and discard the piece of cheese, if used. Taste the soup and correct the seasoning if desired with additional salt or a chicken bouillon cube. You may also find it necessary to correct the saffron seasoning to suit your individual taste.

This soup is good served with a sprinkling of grated Italian cheese and firm crusty bread to dip. A potato saffron soup with meatballs may be made by preparing as above. When the ingredients have cooked for 10 minutes, add some Polpettine (Page 39).

Ann Remembers...
Nothing went to waste in the Sodaro household. When the wedge of Romano or Parmesan cheese became too small and hard to grate anymore, it was saved nonetheless. A small cube of hard cheese would be added to soups and sauces to impart an extra flavor that is difficult to duplicate by merely sprinkling cheese on top.

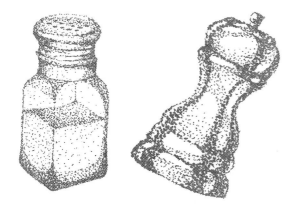

From Ann's Kitchen

Minestra di Patate con Pomodoro
Potato Soup with Tomato

Ann Remembers...

Occasionally my mother or aunt would add poached eggs to this soup to provide their families with a more substantial meal. When the potatoes were cooked, they carefully added an egg per person to the broth, being sure to allow enough space for each egg to poach nicely. This took about 5 minutes. Then one egg at a time was carefully lifted and placed in each bowl, and the soup and grated cheese were passed. This soup is good with toasted bread.

1/4 cup olive oil
1 small onion, chopped
1 large clove garlic, minced
2 tablespoons chopped fresh parsley
1 small piece hard Italian cheese (optional) (Page 41)
4 medium red potatoes, peeled and diced small
1 cup tomato puree, or 1 (8-ounce) can tomatoes, diced
1/2 teaspoon dried basil, or 3 fresh leaves
1/4 teaspoon oregano
Salt and pepper to taste
1 quart water

Heat the oil and add the onion, garlic, parsley and optional cheese. Stir while cooking until the onion is transparent and golden. Add the potatoes and continue stirring for a few minutes. Add the tomato and seasonings. Stir and cook over a low heat for 5 minutes, then add the water. Bring to a boil, reduce the heat, and cook until the potatoes are tender. Remove and discard the piece of cheese, if used, and serve hot.

Zuppa con Pasta e Zucchine
Soup with Pasta and Zucchini

6 small or 4 large zucchini
1/3 cup olive oil
1 medium onion, diced
2 cloves garlic, minced
1 small piece hard Italian cheese (optional) (Page 41)
2 cups fresh or canned tomatoes, peeled and diced,
  or 2 cups tomato puree
2 large basil leaves, or 1/2 teaspoon dried
3 fresh mint leaves, or 1/2 teaspoon dried
2 tablespoons chopped fresh parsley, or 1 teaspoon dried
1/4 teaspoon oregano
1/2 teaspoon sugar
2/3 cup water, or more, if needed
Salt and pepper to taste
1 cup ditalini, or linguini broken into 1-inch pieces
Romano or Parmesan cheese, grated

Scrape the zucchini very lightly. Wash, dice and set aside. Heat the oil, add the onion and cook for about 5 minutes over a medium heat. Add the garlic and optional cheese and sauté another 5 minutes or so. Add the tomato and other ingredients, through the salt and pepper. If canned or fresh tomatoes are used, cook for about 10 minutes, breaking down the fibers with a wooden spoon. Add the diced zucchini and cook for 10 minutes, stirring occasionally.

Add sufficient water to make a soupy mixture, starting with 2/3 cup. Add more if needed. Cook the pasta in sufficient salted boiling water for about 5 minutes. Drain and add to the boiling soup mixture and continue cooking for another 8 to 10 minutes.

Taste to correct the seasoning. Remove and discard the piece of cheese, if used, and serve at once in soup bowls, sprinkling generously with grated cheese. If you prefer to omit the piece of cheese in cooking, stir in 2 tablespoons of grated cheese just before serving.

Ann's Tips...

For those with home vegetable gardens, one item sure to be available in large quantities is zucchini. This recipe was enjoyed in my mother's kitchen and continues to be welcome in mine. The amount of water needed varies depending on whether you use whole tomatoes or tomato puree. In our family, this is a dish that we make with whatever is on hand.

Minestra di Piselli
Quick Pea Soup

1 cup split peas
1 quart water
1/2 cup olive oil
1 small onion, minced
1 clove garlic, minced
1 small piece hard Italian cheese (optional) (Page 41)
1/2 cup diced celery
1/2 cup diced carrots
2 tablespoons chopped fresh parsley
1/8 teaspoon oregano
1/4 teaspoon basil
1/4 teaspoon thyme
1/4 teaspoon onion salt
1/4 teaspoon garlic salt
1/4 teaspoon pepper
2 chicken bouillon cubes
1/2 cup small shells, or other small pasta

Ann Explains...

You don't need three hours and a ham bone to make a tasty pea soup. This recipe may be doubled.

Rinse the peas and add them to boiling water. When the water returns to a boil, reduce to a simmer and cover.

In a smaller pan, heat the olive oil and sauté the onion over a medium heat. When the onion turns golden, add the garlic and optional cheese. Cook 2 or 3 minutes longer. Add the celery and carrots. Cook gently for about 10 minutes, stirring occasionally.

Add these sautéed vegetables and all of the seasonings to the peas. Continue to cook for 1 hour or until the peas have dissolved and thickened. Partially cook the pasta, drain and add to soup about 10 minutes before serving. Taste to correct the seasoning. Remove and discard the piece of cheese, if used, and serve hot.

Pasta e Fagioli
Meatless Pasta and Beans

1/2 cup olive oil
1 medium onion, diced
1 clove garlic, minced
1/2 cup chopped celery
1/2 cup shredded cabbage
1 (1-pound) can tomatoes
2 cans water, or more
1/2 cup split yellow peas
1/2 teaspoon oregano
1/2 teaspoon basil
1/2 teaspoon marjoram
1/4 teaspoon celery salt
1-1/2 teaspoons salt
1/4 teaspoon pepper
1 small bay leaf
1 (16-ounce) can Great Northern beans
1/2 cup cooked small macaroni
2 tablespoons minced fresh parsley
Romano or Parmesan cheese, grated

Ann's Tips...
Meat flavor may be added to this soup by using salt pork or bacon. Reduce the olive oil and use part of the rendered pork fat while sautéing the vegetables.

Heat the oil, add the onion, and cook until it is transparent and beginning to turn golden. Add the garlic, celery and cabbage, and cook over low heat for 6 or 7 minutes, stirring often. Crush or chop the tomatoes and add them to the mixture with their juices. Continue cooking for 5 minutes.

Using the empty tomato can, measure 2 cans of water and add to the pot along with the split peas and all the seasonings except the parsley. Bring it to a boil, then reduce the heat and simmer, covered, for 1 hour. Stir occasionally to keep the peas from sticking to the bottom of the pan. Add the beans and their liquid.

Continue to simmer while separately cooking the pasta until it is *al dente*. Drain and add to the soup. Simmer 10 minutes longer or until thickened. Taste to correct the seasoning. Serve very hot with parsley and grated cheese.

Minestra d'Escarola e Lenticchie
Escarole and Lentil Soup

1 medium onion, chopped
1 large or 2 small cloves garlic, minced
1/4 cup olive oil
2 quarts water
2 sprigs fresh parsley, chopped
1/2 teaspoon oregano, or to taste
1/2 teaspoon basil
Salt and pepper to taste
1 pound lentils
1 head escarole
Romano or Parmesan cheese, grated

Ann Explains...

This recipe is from a dear friend of many years, Angela Giunta.

Sauté the onion and garlic in the olive oil in a large saucepan. Add 2 quarts of water along with the parsley, oregano, basil, salt and pepper. Rinse the lentils and add them to the pot. Cover and cook slowly for 1 hour or until done.

Discard the yellow and tough outer leaves from the escarole, cut the inner leaves into 1-inch pieces, and wash them thoroughly in cold water several times. Cook in a small amount of water in a covered pot for 15 minutes. Stir once or twice during cooking time. Drain and add the escarole to the lentils. Heat through. Serve hot with the grated cheese and a crusty bread such as Pane Pepato di Puglia (Page 55).

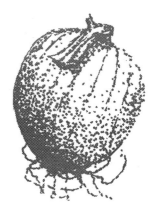

Brodo per Zuppa di Pesce
Broth for Fish Soup

1/3 cup olive oil
1 large clove garlic, minced
1 small piece hard Romano cheese (optional) (Page 41)
1 (16-ounce) can tomato sauce,
  or 1 (16-ounce) can tomatoes, cut small
2 cans water, approximately 1 quart
2 tablespoons chopped fresh parsley, or 1 teaspoon dried
1/2 teaspoon each: oregano, basil, thyme, onion salt, garlic salt
1/4 teaspoon thyme
Salt and pepper to taste

Heat the oil and add the garlic, and optional cheese. Stir while cooking and watch carefully, being sure not to burn the garlic. Have the tomato sauce or cut-up tomatoes ready and add to the pan. If using tomatoes cook for a while to break the fibers before adding the water. Add all the seasonings and cook at a low temperature for 10 to 15 minutes.

Ann's Tips...
This is a basic tomato broth that is suitable for simple fish soups. Onions may be added if desired.

Zuppa di Merluzzo
Whiting Soup

1 recipe Brodo per Zuppa di Pesce
1 large or 2 small merluzzo (whiting)
1 cup small soup pasta, half-cooked and drained

Prepare the broth as directed. Remove the heads and clean the stomach cavity of the fish. Wash well under cold running water. The fish heads may be used if desired. If the fish is large, cut it into 2 or 3 pieces before adding it to the broth. Bring to a boil, then turn down the heat and cook gently for 10 to 12 minutes.

Using a slotted spoon, remove the fish from the broth and allow it to cool on a plate. Remove and discard the skin and the bones. Flake the merluzzo. The soup may be strained if desired. Add the pasta to the broth and complete cooking.

Ann's Tips...
This delicious soup may be served as is or with a garnish of minced parsley and grated cheese. A portion or all of the cooked fish may be returned to the soup a few minutes before it is ready to serve so that it can heat through. The fish also may be set aside for a second course, or fixed as a salad like Insalata di Tonno (Page 34), substituting the whiting for the tuna.

Zuppa con Vermicelli e Vongole
Fish Soup with Vermicelli and Clams

1 recipe Brodo per Zuppa di Pesce (Page 47)
1 cup broken vermicelli
1 or 2 (6-ounce) cans clams
Romano or Parmesan cheese, grated
Fresh parsley, minced, for garnish

Prepare the broth as directed. Cook the vermicelli until half done, drain well and add to the broth with minced clams and their liquid. Cook gently until the pasta is done. Serve very hot in bowls sprinkled with grated cheese and garnished with parsley.

Zuppa di Pesce con Polenta
Fish Soup with Polenta

Cut leftover polenta into small cubes and drop into any of the previous soups. Heat thoroughly and serve as directed.

Ann's Tips...

If you are cooking pasta to be added to other recipes such as soups or casseroles, undercook the pasta since it will undergo further cooking in the final stages of preparation.

Zuppa di Pesce alla Siciliana
Sicilian Fish Soup

3/4 cup olive oil
1 large onion, diced
3 large cloves garlic, whole
1 (28-ounce) can Italian plum tomatoes, cut up
1 cup dry white wine
3 tablespoons chopped fresh parsley, or 1 tablespoon dried
3 or 4 large basil leaves, or 3/4 teaspoon dried
1/2 teaspoon oregano
1/4 teaspoon thyme
1/4 teaspoon marjoram
1/2 teaspoon onion salt
1/2 teaspoon garlic salt
Salt and pepper to taste
2 cans water
1 large merluzzo (whiting)
1 large bass
1 large crab, scrubbed and cracked in 4 pieces
2 or 3 fish heads (optional)
1/2 pound shrimp, shelled and deveined
1/2 pound scallops
1 tall can baby clams and their liquid,
  or 24 baby clams washed and scrubbed
Fresh parsley, minced

Ann's Tips...

When cooking onion or garlic in oil, never let them burn or become too dark as this will impart a bitter flavor to your recipe.

In a large Dutch oven, heat the olive oil and add the onion and garlic. Cook over a moderate heat until the onion becomes transparent and a light golden color. Add the tomatoes and cook while breaking down the tomatoes with a wooden spoon.

When the liquid is reduced to about half, add the wine and all the seasonings. Cook until the wine has evaporated somewhat, then add the water and bring to a boil. Add the merluzzo, bass, crab and optional fish heads. Lower the heat and cook gently for 10 to 12 minutes, or until the fish flakes easily. *(Continued on following page.)*

Sicilian Proverb

⟶⟵

"Lu pisci du mari è
distinatu a cu' si l'avi a
manciari."

•

*(For every fish in the sea,
there is a person destined
to eat it.)*

•

Using a slotted spoon, carefully lift the fish from the soup and set it aside. The broth may be strained at this time if desired. Otherwise, check to be sure no fish skin or large bones remain in the broth. Remove the garlic. Bring to a boil again. Add the shrimp, scallops and clams and cook gently for about 5 minutes.

Meanwhile, remove the bones from the fish, leaving the pieces as large as possible. Return the fish pieces and the crab to the broth and heat thoroughly. Serve in bowls garnished with parsley. Pass a basket of hot crusty bread and enjoy.

Pane e Pizze
Breads and Pizzas

Muddica (Mollica)
Toasted Bread Crumbs

Ann Explains...

In many Sicilian homes, fish-based pasta dishes are not served with grated cheese on top. Instead, each serving is sprinkled with Muddica, or toasted bread crumbs. This is especially true on Christmas Eve, St. Joseph's Day and other meatless observances.

1/3 cup olive oil
2 cloves garlic, through a press or minced
2 cups bread crumbs

Put the oil in a heavy frying pan with the garlic, add the bread crumbs and mix to coat well with the oil. Place on a very slow fire and stir while cooking continuously until the crumbs are a light golden color. Do not allow them to burn. As soon as the crumbs are lightly toasted, remove them from the frying pan to prevent further cooking. Use as suggested in Pasta con le Sarde (Page 82) or sprinkle over any other fish-based pasta dishes. Also good for sprinkling on hot vegetables, with or without a good sprinkling of grated Italian cheese and a little paprika for color. These will keep well in the refrigerator for several weeks in a tightly covered jar.

Pangrattato alle Erbe
Seasoned Bread Crumbs

Ann Remembers...

My parents and grandparents were simple people who were grateful for whatever was provided, and they did not waste anything if they could help it. They especially refused to waste bread. Even when it became too hard to eat, they would break it into small chunks and soak it in a hot broth made from water, seasonings and garlic browned in olive oil. When the bread swelled into billowy sponges it was spooned into a bowl and covered with freshly grated cheese. Called Pane Cotto (cooked bread), it was one of my grandfather's favorite impromptu meals. More often, older bread was simply grated to make seasoned bread crumbs such as this.

4 cups bread crumbs
1 cup grated Romano or Parmesan cheese
4 teaspoons dried parsley
2 teaspoons dried basil
1/2 teaspoon garlic powder
1/2 teaspoon onion salt
1/2 teaspoon salt, or to taste
1/2 teaspoon pepper, or to taste

Mix all the ingredients in a bowl, then store in a tightly covered jar in the refrigerator. Good for breading meat, fish, vegetables, etc., this recipe will keep well.

Pane alla Moda Mia
Bread My Way

2-1/2 pounds flour, approximately 10 cups, divided
1 tablespoon salt
2 tablespoons sugar
2 (1/4-ounce) packets dry yeast mixed with 1 tablespoon
  sugar
1/2 cup warm water
1/2 stick (4 ounces) butter or margarine, divided
1 cup milk
1-1/2 cups warm water
Sesame seeds

Set aside 1/2 cup of the flour. Pour the remaining flour into a large bowl and add the salt and 2 tablespoons of sugar. Stir.

Put the dry yeast in a measuring cup and add the additional tablespoon of sugar and 1/2 cup of warm water. Let stand. After several minutes, stir.

Set aside 1-1/2 teaspoons of butter to use later, then heat together the remainder of the butter and the milk until the butter is melted and the milk is slightly scalded. Do not boil. Add the additional 1-1/2 cups of warm water. Let stand until lukewarm.

Make a well in the center of the bowl of flour and add the milk/butter mixture. Stir slightly and add the yeast mixture. Stir until dry and wet ingredients are blended, then knead by hand for 5 to 8 minutes. If while kneading, the dough becomes too soft and sticks to your hands, use the 1/2 cup of flour that had been set aside.

Use the 1-1/2 teaspoons of reserved butter to grease the ball of dough. Cover with wax paper and a folded dish towel and set in a warm place until doubled in bulk.

Punch down and form into loaves. Place on a cookie sheet or use small bread pans. Let stand to rise again. Sprinkle generously with sesame seeds and bake in a preheated 400-degree oven. Timing will depend on the shape and size of the loaves, but check often after 30 minutes.

Makes 2 small loaves of bread with enough dough left over to make a pizza or some small dinner rolls.

Ann's Tips...

It is difficult for the home chef to duplicate the techniques and resources of a professional baker, but good results are possible with patience and practice. Baking bread is an inexact science. Much depends on the room temperature, the season of the year, the kneading technique of the cook, etc. Sometimes you may find you need more flour than at other times. After making bread just a few times, your hands will be able to feel when it's just right. If you have a mixer with a dough hook, follow the manufacturer's suggestions for mixing.

Calzone
Savory Easter Pie

Ann Explains...

In many regions of Italy, the traditional Calzone is a semicircular turnover. Apparently, it was thought to look like a trouser leg, as the word calzone means pantaloons or trousers. In other variations, it has been adapted into a savory pie, sometimes billed as Pizza Rustica. This is how it is always served in our family on Easter Sunday.

1 pound ricotta, very well drained
2 tablespoons grated Romano cheese
2 large eggs
2 slices salami, diced
2 slices capiccollo, diced
2 slices prosciutto, diced
2 slices provolone, diced
1 link cooked Italian sausage, skin removed and diced
A little pepper
Pasta Frolla (Page 154)

Beat the ricotta and Romano cheeses until smooth and add the eggs, one at a time. Fold in the remaining ingredients. Pour into a pie dish lined with pastry and add a lattice top. Brush with egg wash. Bake in a preheated 375-degree oven for 1 hour.

Cook's Note: This filling is sufficient for a 9-inch pie dish using a flaky dough such as Pasta Frolla (Page 154) or your favorite pie dough. Double the ingredients for a medium 7-inch-by-11-inch dish and triple the recipe for a 9-inch-by-13-inch pan. Using a glass baking dish ensures a nicely browned bottom crust.

Panzarotti
Deep-Fried Pastries

Ann's Tips...

Panzarotti are savory fried turnovers, and may be made with almost any filling that suits your fancy. Instead of the ricotta mixture suggested here, you may fill your Panzarotti with spicy sausage or a combination of vegetables such as tomatoes, onions, olives and capers.

Raised bread dough
Filling for Calzone (Above)
Oil for frying

Roll raised bread dough into thin sheets about 1/8-inch thick. Cut into 4- to 6-inch circles and fill with a heaping tablespoon of filling. Moisten the edges with water, fold over and seal well. Heat vegetable oil until hot and fry panzarotti a few at a time until brown on both sides. Drain on paper towels and serve hot. Delicious.

Pane Pepato di Puglia
Peppered Bread of Puglia

3 slices bacon
1 tablespoon sugar
1 package dry granular yeast
1/4 cup warm water
3 tablespoons margarine
1-1/2 teaspoons salt
1 heaping teaspoon pepper
1 teaspoon dried basil
1/2 cup evaporated milk
1-1/4 cups hot water
5-1/2 cups flour

Brown the bacon slowly. Remove from pan, crumble and set aside. In a small bowl, add the sugar to the yeast and stir in the warm water. Set aside until light and bubbly.

Put the margarine, salt, pepper, basil and milk in a large bowl and pour the hot water over it, stirring to melt margarine. Allow it to stand until lukewarm, then beat in 2 cups of the flour with a wooden spoon.

Add the yeast mixture and the crumbled bacon. Gradually add 3 more cups of flour, working with your hands until a medium dough (not too stiff) is formed. Knead until smooth, about 8 minutes, adding a little more flour if sticky.

Brush the surface with margarine or butter, cover with wax paper and a towel, and set in a warm place to rise for 1 hour or until double in bulk. Knead again and allow to rise an additional 30 minutes. Knead again and shape into a round loaf.

Place in a greased round bread pan or large cake pan. Cover and set in a warm place until double in bulk again. Brush the top with melted butter and bake in a preheated 425-degree oven for 15 minutes. Lower the temperature to 375 degrees and bake 25 minutes longer, or until the bread shrinks from the sides of the pan and is nicely browned.

When the bread is completely cool, cut in half, then cut each half into even slices and wrap securely in aluminum foil.

Ann's Tips...
This is another family recipe from good friend Angela Giunta. If desired, this may be frozen for future use. Each half may be reheated in preheated 350-degree oven when ready to use. It is also delicious when the slices are toasted and buttered.

Bruschetta
Toasted Bread Appetizers

Ann Explains...

Bruschetta comes from the Italian verb "bruscare," which means to toast over coals. However these bread slices are toasted, they are an invitation to create imaginative toppings. In its simplest version, bruschetta is rubbed with a cut piece of garlic, drizzled with a quality olive oil and served warm. Try this topping or create your own.

12 slices baguette-style bread
4 to 5 ripe plum tomatoes
1 clove garlic, through a press or minced
2 teaspoons minced onion
3 fresh basil leaves, chopped
Salt and pepper
Olive oil
Romano cheese, shaved (optional)

Preheat the broiler at least 5 minutes. Slice the bread about 3/8-inches thick and brush both sides lightly with olive oil. Toast the bread on both sides under the broiler. Watch it carefully — this will only take a few minutes. The bread should be lightly toasted. Remove it from the oven and cool. Cut plum tomatoes in half, scoop out the seeds with the tip of a knife and discard. Dice the tomatoes quite small. Toss with garlic, onion, basil, salt and pepper, and enough olive oil to coat well. Spoon topping on each toast slice. If desired, serve with shaved Romano cheese on each bruschetta.

Pane con Aglio e Erbe
Herbed Garlic Bread

1 loaf Italian bread
1 stick butter
2 large cloves garlic, through a press
3/4 cup grated Romano cheese
1 teaspoon dried basil
1 teaspoon oregano
1/2 teaspoon paprika

Slice the loaf of Italian bread in half lengthwise, then make 2-inch diagonal slices almost to the bottom of each half loaf, keeping the bread intact. Melt the butter, add the garlic and stir well. Using a pastry brush, butter the bread on the cut surfaces, including in between the slices. In a small bowl, combine the cheese with the herbs and sprinkle generously on the bread, spreading the mixture to season between slices. Place on cookie sheets and bake in a preheated 425-degree oven until crisp and lightly browned.

Italian Proverb

"Chi vuole un bell'agliaio,
lo pianti di febbraio."

•

(If you want to have good garlic, plant in February.)

•

Mufuletti
Cheese Buns

6 crusty dinner rolls
1/2 cup olive oil
Onion salt
Garlic salt
Pepper
Basil
Oregano
1/2 cup grated Romano or Parmesan cheese
1/2 cup coarsely grated provolone or fontinella cheese
1/2 cup coarsely grated mozzarella cheese
1 pound ricotta, very well drained

Cut the dinner rolls in half and drizzle a teaspoon of olive oil on each side. Sprinkle one side of each roll lightly with onion salt and the second side with garlic salt. Lightly sprinkle pepper, basil and oregano on both sides. Then follow with some of each of the 3 grated cheeses.

Place 1/4 cup ricotta on the bottom half of each roll, then carefully place the top half over the ricotta and press down. Spread a very light coating of olive oil on a baking sheet and place the filled rolls on it.

Cover tightly with aluminum foil and bake in a preheated 350-degree oven for 15 to 20 minutes, or until the ricotta is hot and the other cheeses are melting. Remove from the oven and let stand, covered, for 5 minutes. Serve very hot.

Panelle
Chickpea Fritters

1 pound chickpea flour
1 quart plus 1 cup water
1 teaspoon salt
Pepper
3 or 4 tablespoons minced fresh parsley
Vegetable or olive oil

In a heavy saucepan, put the chickpea flour, water, salt and pepper, and stir until the flour mixture combines well with the water. Place over a medium heat and cook for 15 minutes or more, stirring continuously until a thick paste is achieved. Remove from the heat and stir in the parsley.

Pour into baking pans that have been rinsed off with cold water. Spread the mixture to 1/4-inch thickness and allow to cool completely. Cover with wax paper to keep from drying out.

When completely cold, cut into 2-inch-by-4-inch pieces, lift with a spatula and put into a frying pan covered with hot oil, a few at a time. When the first side is golden brown, turn to brown the second side. Turn out on paper towels to dry, then serve hot.

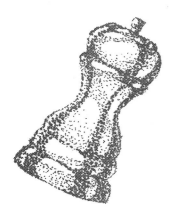

Ann Remembers...

On the Feast of St. Lucy, our family refrained from eating products made of wheat flour. Instead of bread, we were served panelle, which are fritters made of ceci (chickpeas). One of my earliest memories is of coming home from school to a flurry of activity. My grandfather Andrea, hammer in hand, would be pounding ceci enclosed in a cloth sack to pulverize them. Meanwhile, my grandmother Christina would be sifting the pounded beans through a silk screen to accumulate only the finest of the bean flour, which is necessary to make a smooth panella. Blessedly, it eventually became possible to buy commercially milled ceci flour. In memory of St. Lucy and the Sodaro family's devotion to this tradition, I offer you my Aunt Carmela's recipe for panelle.

Dough for Pizza

1 ounce fresh compressed yeast
1 tablespoon sugar
1/2 cup canned milk
1-1/2 cups warm water
1 teaspoon salt
3 tablespoons vegetable oil
4 cups flour, or more, as needed
White or yellow corn meal

Crumble the cake of yeast in a cup, sprinkle with the sugar and stir slightly. Allow to rest for 5 to 10 minutes, or until yeast is liquefied.

Pour the canned milk into a large mixing bowl and add the water. If canned milk is not available, use 1 cup scalded whole milk and change the water measurement to 1 cup lukewarm water. Whatever combination you use, be sure the mixture is lukewarm before adding the yeast to it.

To the water and milk, add the salt, oil and 2 cups of the flour. Beat well with a wooden spoon. Add the yeast and beat again. Cover and let rise for 5 to 10 minutes.

Add an additional 2- to 2-1/2 cups of the flour, mixing until a medium soft dough is formed. Knead the dough until smooth. The dough may be a little sticky. Brush the top with a little vegetable oil, turn over and brush the second side with oil. Cover with plastic wrap, then with a terry-cloth dish towel. Set in a draft-free area. (A cold oven works well.) Allow dough to rise until it is double in bulk. This may take 1-1/2 to 2 hours.

Punch the dough down and turn it out onto a floured surface. Knead a few minutes, then divide the dough into 2 pieces. Form into balls and cover for 5 to 10 minutes.

Pizzas

Coat two 15-1/2-inch-by-10-inch cookie pans with sides (jelly roll pans) with olive oil and sprinkle with corn meal. Take one ball of the dough, place on a floured surface and flatten it with the heels of your hands while stretching and pulling. Pick up the dough and pull and stretch some more. Place it in the center of the pan, pressing and pulling the dough toward the edges of the pan.

The dough will resist. Let it rest while working the second ball of dough. Follow the same steps. Then go back to the first pan and stretch the dough more. Continue this method with the 2 pans until the dough has been stretched to the 4 corners of the pans.

Spread with your favorite pizza sauce. Sprinkle with a combination of coarsely grated mozzarella and fontinella cheeses and a good sprinkling of grated Romano cheese. Next sprinkle oregano and some dried basil over all. Lastly, drizzle with 2 or 3 tablespoons of olive oil.

Bake on the lower rack of a preheated 500-degree oven for about 30 minutes, or until nicely browned on the bottom. It may be necessary to turn the pans around once. Heat varies among ovens, so check often after 20 minutes.

Sauce for Pizza

1 tablespoon virgin olive oil
2 tablespoons minced onion
1 small clove garlic, minced
1 (16-ounce) can tomato sauce or puree
1/2 teaspoon sugar, or to taste
4 fresh basil leaves, minced
1/8 teaspoon dried mint
Salt (optional)

Ann's Tips...
Before adding salt to your pizza sauce, taste it first, as some canned tomato products already have salt added. If you need salt, add 1/2 teaspoon and taste again before adding more.

In a small saucepan, heat the olive oil and cook the onion gently until it begins to soften. Add the garlic and sauté 1 to 2 minutes more. Add the remaining ingredients. Simmer slowly for 15 minutes. Store until ready to make pizza. *(Continued on following page.)*

Additional Toppings

The traditional Neapolitan-style pizza with tomato sauce and grated cheeses is much loved, but consider some of these toppings in addition to or instead of the traditional.

Salsiccia Casalinga (Page 114)
Sautéed onions
Peperoni Rossi Arrostiti (Page 12)
Sautéed mushrooms
Zucchine alla Griglia (Page 15)
Anchovies
Pesto (Page 71)

For the last variation, use pesto instead of tomato sauce and top with thinly sliced plum tomatoes and dollops of ricotta or a sprinkling of mozzarella.

Sicilian Proverb

"Nun c'è megghiu sarsa di la fami."

•

(Hunger is the best sauce.)

•

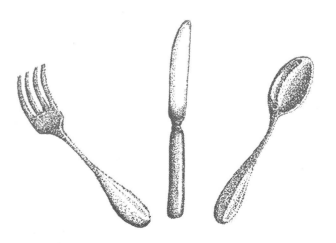

Sughi, Paste e Riso
Sauces, Pastas and Rice

Ann's Tips...

A hand-cranked pasta machine is helpful in making pasta at home. It has various settings for different thicknesses of pasta. If you do not have one, don't despair. Just be sure to roll your dough thin enough, approximately 1/16 of an inch.

3 cups all-purpose flour
4 eggs
1 teaspoon salt

Sift the flour onto a pastry board and make a well in the center. Break the eggs into the well and add the salt. Mix the eggs into the flour with a fork or with the fingertips and work the dough well. Knead for 10 minutes, or until it is smooth and pliable. Let it rest about 20 minutes, covered with a cloth. Roll the dough out into a thin sheet. Cut into desired shapes.

Pasta Verde
Basil Noodles

Ann Remembers...

Each year in early summer, my good friend, the late Pauline Jo Cusimano, would make a "love gift" to Tony and me of several basil plants. It was a delightful custom that we both looked forward to. Tony would carefully and lovingly plant them in an herb plot close to my kitchen door. From this vantage point, I enjoyed watching them grow into hardy, healthy plants. The "love gift" lasted all year long. Through the summer I would make daily trips to pick fresh leaves for our evening meal. Through the winter months, we enjoyed the basil that I had set aside for drying and freezing. These noodles were the result of one of my fall basil harvesting experiments. They look like spinach noodles and may be served with a fresh marinara sauce.

1-1/3 cups fresh basil leaves, firmly packed
2 eggs
2 tablespoons water
4 teaspoons corn oil
1/2 teaspoon salt
2 cups flour, or more

Wash the basil leaves, drain well and dry on paper towels. Measure the basil and put into a blender together with the other ingredients except the flour. Blend on high until all the basil leaves have combined well. Pour into a bowl and start mixing in the flour to absorb all the liquid.

Knead in the last of the flour by hand, adding more than the 2 cups if necessary, until a firm dough is formed with no flour visible. Cover and allow to rest for 1/2 hour. Roll out using a pasta machine and cut into fettuccine size, about 1/4-inch wide. Cook in salted boiling water just until they rise to the surface. Do not overcook. Drain well and serve with sauce and grated cheese.

Cappelletti
Little Hats

1 pound boneless chicken breasts
1/3 pound pork tenderloin
Sweet butter, approximately 2 sticks
Grated rind of 2 lemons
1/2 pound Parmesan cheese, grated
1 teaspoon cinnamon, or to taste
1 teaspoon nutmeg, or to taste
1 recipe Egg Pasta (Page 64)

Sauté the chicken breasts and pork tenderloin in a portion of the butter. Finely grind both using a meat grinder or food processor. Add the remaining butter and all the other ingredients through the nutmeg. You need enough butter to ensure a very moist mixture. Add more if the ingredients seem too dry.

Prepare the Egg Pasta. Roll out the dough to 1/16-inch thickness and cut it into circles 1-1/2- to 2-inches in diameter. Do not let the dough dry out. Work with it in divided portions, keeping the remaining dough covered. Place a scant 1/2 teaspoon of filling in each circle and shape immediately into "little hats." This is done by folding the circle in half and securely sealing the edge. Pick up the semicircle using both hands with the rounded edge downward. Holding each end between thumb and index finger, turn the edges inward until they meet and firmly pinch them together. Curl the edge up slightly.

Ann Remembers…

Some people have a special way of saying "Happy Holidays!" For many years, our lifelong friend, Josephine Salerno Lucatorto, would present us with one of the most awaited gifts of the season — her homemade cappelletti. Making them is a Salerno family tradition, and with many hands working together, they would produce these delicious morsels by the thousands! The version shown here has been adapted to smaller proportions from the recipes of Josephine and her sister, Molly Ferrari.

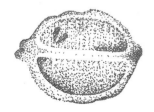

Tortellini di Bologna
Bolognese Stuffed Pasta

3 pounds center-cut pork chops
1 chicken breast
1 or 2 cloves garlic, sliced
Salt and pepper to taste
1 pound prosciutto
3/4 pound mortadella
1 pound Parmesan cheese, grated
4 eggs
4 egg yolks
1 teaspoon nutmeg
3 recipes Egg Pasta (Page 64)

Ann Explains...

Tortellini somewhat resemble cappelletti in shape, although legend has it that the creator of tortellini fashioned them after Venus' navel. This recipe was a regional specialty of another very dear friend, the late Nella Scalise. She also mass-produced these for family and friends. Like cappelletti, these are often served in a rich chicken broth. They may also be tossed with butter and cheese or served with a sauce of your choice.

Fry the pork chops together with the chicken breast, garlic, salt and pepper. Discard the garlic, the pork chop bones and the skin from the chicken breast. Grind all meats — pork, chicken, prosciutto, mortadella — about 4 times, or until very fine.

Add the cheese, eggs, egg yolks, nutmeg, and more salt and pepper. Mix or knead together until the mixture clings together without crumbling. If necessary, add another egg. Refrigerate any portion you are not using immediately.

Make the Egg Pasta, adding 1/2 teaspoon of nutmeg for each recipe of the dough if desired. Roll dough to 1/16-inch thickness and cut into 2-inch discs, or smaller, if desired. Do not allow the pasta to dry out.

As each piece of dough is rolled out, begin to make tortellini. Place approximately 1/2 teaspoon of filling on each circle. Fold in half to make half moons. If pasta is drying too quickly, use a very slight amount of water on the edge to seal.

Wrap the half moon around your little finger or your index finger with the rounded edge upward. Connect the 2 tips by pressing with your thumb. Turn the sealed outer edge over to form a cuff. Slip them off your finger and make sure the ends are firmly pinched together. Allow to dry before cooking.

Moglio d'Aglio
Fresh Tomato and Garlic Sauce

4 large fresh ripe tomatoes
2 cloves garlic, through a press
Fresh minced or dried basil or oregano, to taste
2 tablespoons olive oil
1 teaspoon salt
1/4 teaspoon pepper

Remove the skin from the tomatoes as directed for Salsa di Pomodoro (Page 68), then cut them into small pieces in a bowl and add the rest of the ingredients. Let stand at room temperature for about an hour. This is an uncooked sauce.

Conserva di Pomodoro
Seasoned Tomato Puree for the Freezer

3 pounds tomatoes, preferably plum
1 medium carrot
1 medium onion
1 large rib celery
4 or 5 large basil leaves, plus extra for freezing
Salt

Wash and cut up the tomatoes; slice the carrot, onion and celery into small pieces; and place all in a pan together with the basil. Stir, pressing the tomatoes with the back of a wooden spoon to release some juices. Set on a medium heat and bring to a boil. Stir often to prevent sticking or scorching. Cook until most of the liquid evaporates, but the tomatoes are still moist. This is best achieved by cooking in small batches. If too much liquid remains, remove some with a dipper and store for use in soups and sauces. Cool the tomato mixture, then pass it through a food mill, being sure to press out all the vegetables. Season with 1/4 teaspoon salt per cup of sauce and store in freezer bags with a fresh basil leaf in each.

Ann's Tips...

For those times when a dish of pasta sounds good but you don't want to devote long hours to cooking, I offer this recipe shared with me by a good Sicilian cook, Grace Licata. Preparations such as this are used throughout Sicily and are referred to as "ammogghiu." Besides using on pasta, it can be spooned over grilled meat, fish or eggplant. It's also delicious for dipping bread. In the summer when tomatoes are abundant try tossing this raw tomato sauce on hot pasta for a different treat.

Ann's Tips...

From the bounty of our summer garden I make a tomato puree which I keep in 1- and 2-cup portions in the freezer. This is handy for many recipes and helps to extend my enjoyment of the garden.

Salsa di Pomodoro
Fresh Tomato Sauce with Tomato Bits

1-1/2 to 2 pounds tomatoes
1/3 cup olive oil
1 medium onion, chopped
1 large clove garlic, minced
6 large mushrooms, sliced (optional)
2 or 3 fresh basil leaves, chopped, or 1/2 teaspoon dried
1 tablespoon chopped fresh parsley
1/4 teaspoon oregano
2 tablespoons grated Romano or Parmesan cheese (optional)
1 teaspoon sugar (optional)
Salt and pepper to taste

Ann's Tips...

The acidity of tomatoes varies depending on the variety and the soil in which they were grown. When preparing sauces using fresh tomatoes, you may add a little sugar to cut the acidity. After the sauce simmers awhile, taste to decide if more sugar is needed.

Plunge washed tomatoes into boiling water and allow them to remain no more than 1 minute. Run cold water over them, then remove the skins. Cut the tomatoes in half and squeeze the seeds and juice into a pot. Dice the tomato pulp and add a little more than half of it to the juice. Set the rest of the tomato pulp aside until later.

Cook the tomato juice over a medium heat, stirring occasionally, until it is reduced to about half. Put it through a strainer or food mill, squeezing out as much of the pulp as possible. Heat the oil in a skillet, add the onion and garlic and cook for 1 or 2 minutes. Add the mushrooms if desired and cook another 2 minutes.

Now add the strained tomato sauce and the balance of the diced tomatoes and bring to a boil. Add all remaining ingredients and cook over a medium heat until the sauce is of a medium-thick consistency. This sauce is good over pastas or vegetable dishes.

Variation One (Quick Sauce)

For a quick sauce, use all of the ingredients above except mushrooms. If desired, the onion may be omitted and garlic increased to 2 large cloves. Wash the tomatoes and remove the skins as directed. Dice or chop all of the tomatoes in a bowl, juice and pulp together.

Fresh Tomato Sauce with Tomato Bits

Heat the oil and add the onion and garlic (or garlic alone) and brown to a golden color. Add the tomatoes and seasonings and cook over a medium-high heat until the sauce is of the desired consistency. This is best done in a broad pan such as a large skillet. It should not cook too long or it will become dark, and this sauce should be red in color.

Variation Two (Quick Sauce)

Same as above, except substitute 1 (28-ounce) can of plum tomatoes for the fresh tomatoes.

Salsa del Cacciatore
Hunter-Style Sauce

2 (1-pound) cans or 1 (28-ounce) can plum tomatoes, chopped
2 tablespoons olive oil
2 tablespoons butter
1/2 pound fresh mushrooms, sliced
1 large onion, diced
1 medium green pepper, diced, or half green and half red pepper
2 cloves garlic, minced
1/4 cup sherry or light dry white wine
1/4 teaspoon each: oregano, thyme, rosemary
1/4 cup grated Romano or Parmesan cheese (optional)
Salt and pepper to taste
2 chicken bouillon cubes (optional)
3 tablespoons minced fresh parsley

Chop the tomatoes, reserving the liquid. Heat the oil and butter in a saucepan and, when hot, add half the sliced mushrooms. Stir while cooking over a medium-high heat until lightly golden. Remove with a slotted spoon and repeat with the balance of the mushrooms. Set aside.

Lower the heat and add the onion and green pepper, cooking for 5 to 8 minutes. Watch closely; do not let them burn. Add the garlic and, after 2 minutes, add the wine and the liquid drained from the tomatoes. Continue to cook until reduced by half.

Add the tomatoes to the pan and cook for 10 minutes. Add the mushrooms and all the other seasonings except for the parsley and cook slowly until the mixture is quite thick. Stir in the parsley and serve over the pasta of your choice.

Pesto
Basil-Parsley Sauce

3 or 4 cloves garlic
1/2 cup pine nuts or chopped walnuts
1 cup olive oil
2 cups firmly packed fresh parsley leaves
2 cups firmly packed fresh basil leaves
3/4 cup grated Romano or Parmesan cheese
Salt and pepper to taste

In a blender or food processor, mix the garlic, nuts and some of the olive oil into a paste. Chop the parsley and basil and add to the blender together with the cheese. Continue to blend, adding the remaining oil gradually. Add salt and pepper. May be stored in the refrigerator in a tightly covered jar with olive oil to cover.

Ann Explains…

Basil is associated with the area of Italy around Genoa where it flourishes in unrivaled abundance. Pesto is a green sauce used in a variety of ways, but especially with homemade egg noodles and other pasta dishes. Its combination of basil, oil, garlic and pine nuts produces a flavor and aroma that adds something special to a dish. This version also relies on the flavor of fresh parsley. Use the flat-leaf Italian variety if possible.

Polpette
Meatballs

1/3 cup bread crumbs
1/3 cup grated Romano or Parmesan Cheese
1/3 cup water
1 clove garlic, through a press or minced
1 tablespoon minced onion, or 1 teaspoon dehydrated minced
1 teaspoon salt
1/4 teaspoon pepper
2 tablespoons chopped fresh parsley
2 eggs
3/4 pound ground round steak
1/4 pound ground pork

Combine the crumbs, cheese and water. Add the seasonings, eggs and meat. Mix well. Divide the mixture into 12 to 15 meatballs. Brown in hot olive oil and add to your favorite sauce recipe.

Ann's Tips...

You may use 1 pound of ground round in this recipe and omit the pork if you prefer.

Polpette Ripiene
Stuffed Meatballs

1 recipe Polpette (above)
1 large egg, hard-boiled and cut into 8 wedges
2 or 3 green onions, cut into 1-1/2-inch pieces
8 pieces Italian cheese, cut into 1-1/2-by-1/8-inch strips
2 slices prosciutto, cut into 4 strips each

Mix the ingredients for Polpette. Divide the mixture into 8 portions. Wet the palm of your hand and press a portion of the meat mixture flat (the size of a hamburger). In the center of this place a piece of egg, onion, cheese and prosciutto. Fold the meat over the filling, being sure to eliminate all open spaces. Form into the shape of a small football. Brown in hot olive oil and add to your favorite sauce recipe.

Ann Explains...

At many Italian tables, pasta is the Primo Piatto, a first course preceding the entree. But the addition of a substantial meat serving, such as these stuffed meatballs or the beef rolls that follow, turns the pasta course into a main event.

Braciole di Manzo in Salsa Rossa
Sicilian Beef Rolls for Sauce

1 cup bread crumbs
1/4 cup grated Romano or Parmesan cheese
1/2 teaspoon each: salt, basil
1/4 teaspoon each: pepper, oregano
1 tablespoon chopped fresh parsley
1/4 cup olive oil, plus additional oil for frying
1 small clove garlic, through a press or minced
8 to 10 very thin slices sirloin-tip steaks
3 hard-boiled eggs
2 or 3 strips bacon, cut into 1-inch lengths
16 to 20 (1/2-inch-by-1-1/2-inch) strips caciocavallo cheese
4 green onions, cut into 1-inch lengths, or 1 small onion, thinly sliced
1 pound pasta

Prepare a dressing by combining the bread crumbs in a bowl with the grated cheese, salt, pepper and herbs. Add the olive oil and garlic. Mix well to coat the bread crumbs with oil.

On wax paper, lay out the steaks and spread the dressing over them, dividing the mixture evenly. Cut the hard-boiled eggs into halves lengthwise, then cut each half into thirds.

Place 2 pieces each of egg, bacon, cheese and onion on each steak, at the end closest to you. Roll the steaks tightly, starting from the end closest to you. Secure with round wooden picks.

Heat 1/3 to 1/2 cup of oil in a heavy frying pan and brown the meat rolls. Turn carefully to brown on all sides. Remove the meat rolls to a saucepan, and in the remaining oil prepare a spaghetti sauce of your choice. Pour the sauce over the meat rolls in the saucepan. Bring to a boil then turn down to a simmer, cover and cook gently for 2 hours, or until the meat is fork-tender.

Ann Explains…

Braciole is popular throughout Italy and has many variations. Serve the sauce from this recipe over pasta, accompanied by the meat rolls. (Be sure to remove the wooden picks from the meat before serving!) Pass the grated cheese and any additional sauce, and enjoy!

Tagliatelle Verdi con Ragù di Carne
Green Noodles with Meat Sauce

1/4 cup olive oil

1 medium onion, diced

2 cloves garlic, through a press or minced

1 pound lean ground beef, sirloin or round

1/2 pound lean ground pork, shoulder or butt

1 (28-ounce) can plum tomatoes

1 (28-ounce) can tomato puree

2 (6-ounce) cans tomato paste

4 tomato paste cans water

2 teaspoons salt, or to taste

2 teaspoons sugar

1/2 teaspoon pepper

1 teaspoon basil

1/2 teaspoon oregano

1/4 teaspoon mint (optional)

1/4 teaspoon fennel seeds, ground (Page 113)

1/4 teaspoon ground cloves, or to taste

1/4 teaspoon nutmeg, or to taste

Dash cinnamon (optional)

2 tablespoons chopped fresh parsley

Grated Romano cheese

1 pound spinach noodles (tagliatelle or fettuccine)

Ann's Tips…

Often at Christmas time I serve a course of green noodles with a rich meat sauce. In this way I introduce the Christmas colors to my table with the green noodles, red sauce and white grated cheese. Since these are also the colors of the Italian flag they make a festive addition to any Italian dinner or buffet.

Heat the oil over a medium heat and sauté the onion until soft and golden in color. Add the garlic and continue cooking for about 1 minute while stirring with a wooden spoon. Add the ground meats and cook until the meat begins to brown.

Put the plum tomatoes in a food mill or strainer and press the tomatoes through. Add to the meat and cook about 15 minutes. Add the tomato puree, tomato paste and water. Add all seasonings, including 2 tablespoons of grated cheese, and bring to a boil, then cover and turn to a simmer. Cook 2-1/2 hours, stirring often.

Green Noodles with Meat Sauce

Cook noodles *al dente* and drain well. Return to the pan, add a small portion of the sauce to the noodles and combine. Arrange on a serving platter or individual dishes and cover with additional sauce and sprinkle with grated cheese.

Sugo con Salsiccia Nostrana
Sauce with Italian Sausage

A delicious spaghetti sauce may be prepared using Italian sausage for the meat base. Simply brown sausage in a pan and remove to a dish. Sausage need not be completely cooked at this point. Remove all but 1/4 cup of the drippings from the pan and into this add onions and garlic and sauté to a golden color. Proceed from there, using a simple recipe for a sauce of your choice and, of course, substituting the sausage for any meat called for. The sausage is cooked for the entire preparation time. Serve the sauce over a pasta of your choice, accompanied by 1 or 2 links of sausage. Pass the grated cheese.

Ann's Tips...

When cooking sauces, it is sometimes difficult to maintain a gentle simmer, even at the lowest heat setting. Lifting the cover and stirring frequently is helpful. A simmer ring, which can be purchased at a kitchenware store, is another way to ensure a very slow simmer.

Pasta 'Ncasciata
Baked Pasta, Sicilian-Style

1/4 cup olive oil
1-1/2 pounds lean pork shoulder or butt, in 1 piece
1 medium onion, diced
2 cloves garlic, through a press or minced
1 (28-ounce) can plum tomatoes
1 (28-ounce) can tomato puree
2 (6-ounce) cans tomato paste
6 tomato paste cans water
2 teaspoons salt
2 teaspoons sugar
1/2 teaspoon pepper
1/2 teaspoon oregano
1 teaspoon basil
2 tablespoons chopped fresh parsley
Dash ground cloves
Dash nutmeg
1/4 teaspoon fennel seeds, ground (Page 113)
1/4 cup grated Romano or Parmesan cheese
1 medium cauliflower
Olive oil for frying
1 pound mostaccioli
Additional grated Romano or Parmesan cheese for layering

Ann Explains…
Many families around
Palermo make some version
of Pasta 'Ncasciata. The
common elements seem to
be a quill-shaped or tubular
pasta such as mostaccioli or
penne layered with a rich
ragu and various cheeses
and vegetables. This is
our family's version.

Heat the oil over a medium heat. Add the pork and brown on all sides. Set aside. Sauté the onion until soft and golden in color. Add the garlic and continue cooking about 1 minute while stirring with a wooden spoon. Put plum tomatoes in food blender and chop for a few seconds, or strain tomatoes through a food mill or strainer. Add to the onion and cook for about 15 minutes. Add the puree, tomato paste and water.

Add all seasonings, including the 1/4 cup grated cheese. Return the pork to the pot, bring to a boil, then turn to a low heat. Simmer for 2-1/2 hours, or until the meat is fork-tender. Stir often. Remove the meat, cut it into small pieces and set aside.

Baked Pasta, Sicilian-Style

Break the cauliflower into small florets and cook it in salted water about 12 minutes. Drain well and cool. Sauté the cauliflower in hot olive oil. Set aside. Cook the pasta according to instructions on the package.

In a large baking or roasting pan, measuring at least 10-inches-by-16-inches-by-3-inches, spoon enough sauce to cover the bottom of the pan. Add a layer of mostaccioli, then a layer of pork, sauce and cauliflower. Sprinkle generously with grated cheese. Continue layering until all the ingredients are used up. The top layers should be sauce and cheese. Bake in a preheated 350-degree oven for 20 to 30 minutes, or until it is hot and bubbly. Serve with additional sauce and grated cheese.

This recipe may be prepared in advance and refrigerated, then baked when needed. The baking period will be longer, due to all the ingredients being cold.

Ann Remembers...
On the Feast of St. Lucy, when our family abstained from pasta and other products made with wheat flour, my mother always served Riso 'Ncasciato. She prepared this by replacing the mostaccioli with one pound of rice.

Pasta alla Palermitana
Pasta, Palermo-Style

1/3 cup olive oil
1 medium onion, diced
1 large clove garlic, minced
1 (28-ounce) can crushed tomatoes
1/4 teaspoon oregano
1/2 teaspoon sugar
Salt and pepper to taste
3 large basil leaves, chopped, or 1/2 teaspoon dried basil
1 tablespoon chopped fresh parsley
1 recipe Fried Eggplant (recipe follows)
1 pound linguine or spaghetti
Romano or Parmesan cheese, grated
Basil sprigs for garnish

Ann Remembers...

Pasta alla Palermitana was served often in our home when I was growing up. When my husband and I visited Palermo one summer we found this dish featured in every restaurant we visited, if not as an entree, then as a side dish. It may be accompanied by a green salad, but good crusty bread is a "must."

Heat the oil, add the onion and cook over a medium heat for 3 to 4 minutes, or until transparent. Add the garlic, cook another 1 to 2 minutes, then add the tomatoes and bring to a gentle boil. Add the oregano, sugar, salt and pepper and cook until the sauce is almost done. Add the basil and parsley for the last few minutes.

Prepare the Fried Eggplant. Cook pasta *al dente* and drain well. Return to the pan, add a small portion of the sauce to the pasta and combine. Place pasta on individual dishes, cover with remaining sauce and sprinkle with grated cheese. Top each serving with a few slices of eggplant, tuck a few sprigs of basil around each dish, and serve.

Pasta, Palermo-Style

Fried Eggplant

1 medium eggplant
1/2 cup olive oil, or more, as needed
Romano or Parmesan cheese, grated
Fresh chopped or dried basil

Peel eggplant and cut it in half, then cut each half into lengthwise slices, 1/4-inch thick. Sprinkle the slices with salt and place on a plate in layers between sheets of paper towel. Put a heavy bowl or something else of weight on top and allow to rest for 1/2 hour.

Squeeze several slices at a time to remove excess moisture. This may be done with paper towels. Brown the slices in hot olive oil and place on paper towels. When all the eggplant is cooked, arrange in layers, sprinkling each layer with cheese and basil.

Linguine con Aglio ed Olio
Linguine with Garlic and Oil

1/3 cup olive oil
3 medium cloves garlic, through a press or minced
2 tablespoons chopped fresh parsley, or 2 teaspoons dried
1/2 teaspoon salt, or to taste
1/8 teaspoon pepper
1/2 pound linguine, cooked
1/3 to 1/2 cup grated Romano or Parmesan cheese
Red pepper flakes (optional)

Heat the oil, add the garlic and gently sauté for 2 or 3 minutes until fragrant. Do not brown or burn the garlic, or it will take on a bitter taste. Stir in the parsley, salt and pepper and set aside.

Prepare the pasta and drain well. Towards the end of the cooking time, reheat the oil carefully and toss it with the drained linguine and cheese, coating evenly. Sprinkle with a few red pepper flakes if desired or offer it at the table for individual use.

Ann's Tips...

As a variation, prepare Pasta con Vongole by adding 1 (6-ounce) can of undrained clams when stirring in the parsley and seasonings. Be sure to heat thoroughly before tossing with pasta.

Rigatoni al Sugo di Tonno
Rigatoni with Fresh Tuna Sauce

1 recipe Herb Mixture (recipe follows)
1-1/2 to 2 pounds fresh tuna, in 1 piece
1/4 to 1/3 cup olive oil
1 small onion, chopped
1 large clove garlic, minced
1 (28-ounce) can plum tomatoes
1 (6-ounce) can tomato paste
2 tomato paste cans of water
2 teaspoons salt
1 teaspoon sugar
2 large fresh basil leaves, minced, or 1/2 teaspoon dried
Sprig fresh mint, or 1/4 teaspoon dried (optional)
1/2 teaspoon oregano
1/4 teaspoon pepper
1 tablespoon chopped fresh parsley
1/2 small bay leaf
1 pound rigatoni or other tubular pasta
Romano or Parmesan cheese, grated

Ann's Tips...

Tuna is found in the oceans of most temperate and warm climates, including the waters around Sicily, and they can weigh as much as 1,500 pounds! We used to anticipate the appearance of fresh tuna at our markets around July and August. Today it can be found most of the year, sometimes as frozen tuna steaks. For this dish, it is preferable to have one thick piece of tuna, 1-1/2- to 2-inches thick, rather than thinner slices or steaks. You may not see these larger cuts of tuna in the market, so ask!

Prepare the herb mixture. Wash the tuna and pat it dry. Make slits over the surface of the fish on both sides. Stuff each slit with some of the herb mixture. Heat the oil in a skillet and brown the tuna on all sides. When brown, remove it to a saucepan in which the sauce is to be cooked, and set aside.

Add the onion to the oil remaining in the skillet and cook over a moderate heat for about 5 minutes. Add the garlic and continue cooking until the onion is soft and golden. Drain the tomatoes, add the liquid to the onion/garlic mixture in the skillet and cook slowly. Chop the tomatoes in small pieces to break the fibers and add to the skillet. Cook for about 15 minutes, then add the tomato paste, which has been diluted with the 2 tomato paste cans of water, and cook 5 minutes longer.

Pour this mixture over the tuna in the saucepan and add all the remaining ingredients through the bay leaf. Bring to a boil, reduce to a simmer, cover and cook for 2 hours.

Rigatoni with Fresh Tuna Sauce

More water may be added if needed. Dry white wine may be substituted for some of the water, and will enhance the flavor of the sauce.

Cook the pasta *al dente* and drain well. Remove the tuna from the sauce, slice and set aside. Return the pasta to the pan, add a small portion of the sauce and combine. Arrange on individual dishes and cover with additional sauce. Top with tuna slices, sprinkle with grated cheese and serve.

Herb Mixture

3 large basil leaves, minced, or 1 teaspoon dried
4 or 5 mint leaves, minced, or 1/2 teaspoon dried
1 teaspoon oregano
2 tablespoons chopped fresh parsley, or 2 teaspoons dried
1 large or 2 small cloves garlic, chopped
1 teaspoon salt
1/4 teaspoon pepper

Combine all ingredients and mix well.

Ann's Tips...

When cooking pasta, be sure to use enough water — about 4 quarts for 1 pound of pasta. Let the water come to a boil, then add the salt just before adding the pasta.

Pasta con le Sarde
Pasta with Fresh Sardine Sauce

1 medium cauliflower
1 large fennel bulb with leaves
1 large onion, diced
Water
1/2 cup olive oil
2 cloves garlic, minced
1 can anchovy fillets
1/8 teaspoon Spanish saffron powder
Salt and pepper to taste
2 tablespoons flour
1-1/2 pounds fresh sardines,
    or 2 cans quality whole sardines packed in olive oil
2 tablespoons pine nuts
1 pound mostaccioli
Toasted Bread Crumbs (Page 52)

Ann Remembers…

This was always served as our evening meal on March 19, the Feast of St. Joseph. As with Pasta 'Ncasciata, you can go from village to village in Sicily and find different versions of this recipe. In addition to the sardines, all the recipes call for anchovies, pine nuts and fennel (some use only the fennel leaves, others also add chopped fennel bulb). Many cooks add white seedless raisins, tomato paste, onion or garlic. The use of bread crumbs, toasted or plain, is common. This recipe is how the dish was prepared by my grandmother and mother, who were from Termini Imerese. It is different from the others I've seen because it depends on Spanish saffron for its flavor. Perhaps this may stem from some distant Spanish ancestors in our family background.

Select firm white cauliflower and cut it into small florets. Wash and set aside. Select only the fine tender fennel leaves from the fennel bulb, discarding tough or brown leaves. Measure 1 cup packed, then wash the leaves and cut into pieces, 1-inch or less.

Put the onion into a 1-quart saucepan with 2 tablespoons water. Measure olive oil, and reserve 2 tablespoons for preparing the sardines. Add the remainder to the onions. Bring to a boil, then reduce to a medium heat and cook uncovered until the water is evaporated and the onion becomes transparent and golden. Add the garlic and cook for 2 or 3 minutes.

Drain the anchovies, reserving the oil, cut up the fillets and add to the pan. Stir while cooking until they are dissolved into a paste. Add 2 cups of water and the saffron. Season lightly with salt and pepper. Add the fennel leaves, bring to a slow boil and cook gently for 10 minutes. Add the cauliflower and continue cooking 10 or 12 minutes. Stir the flour into the oil reserved from the anchovies. Add to the vegetable mixture, stir and cook a few minutes.

Pasta with Fresh Sardine Sauce

Now you may add the fresh or canned sardines. (Instructions for preparing fresh sardines follow.)

Add the fish together with the pine nuts to the cauliflower and fennel mixture. Stir gently to combine the flavors. Taste to check seasoning. Cover and keep hot over a very low heat while the pasta is cooking.

Cook pasta *al dente* and drain well. Return to the pan, add half the sauce, combine and heat through. Arrange on a serving platter and cover with remaining sauce. Sprinkle with bread crumbs.

Preparing Fresh Sardines

If you are using fresh sardines, remove the heads and clean the cavities, then wash. (The next step requires a little patience and can be omitted.) Using a small sharp knife, remove the skin of the sardine under cold running water by lifting a portion of it with the point of the knife and then pulling it away from the flesh.

Remove the flesh from the bone by running your thumb along the spine edge of the fish, keeping the pieces as large as possible. Put the fish in a small saucepan. Add water to cover and the 2 tablespoons of reserved oil. Season with salt and pepper and cook gently until the fish turns white and flakes easily.

Ann' Tips...

Saffron is an acquired taste. It is better to start with a little and add more if it is desired. Some saffron is sold in threadlike form. This can be pulverized by putting some between sheets of wax paper and rubbing it back and forth with the back of a tablespoon. Although only the leaves of the fennel are used in this recipe, the bulb makes a delicious addition to an antipasto tray when cut into wedges and crisped in the refrigerator. Sardines purchased for this dish should be large to medium in size. If they are too small, they are difficult to work with. Finding fresh sardines at all these days can be a challenge! Try locating a fish market that serves an ethnic population like the Italian or Greek communities.

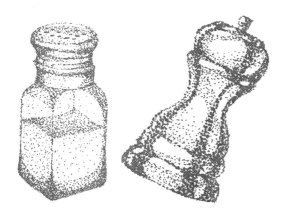

Pasta di San Giuseppe
St. Joseph's Spaghetti

2 heads cauliflower or broccoli
Olive oil for sautéing
2 cloves garlic, minced
4 medium artichokes
Lemon juice
Salt to taste
1 pound spaghetti
3 to 4 cups homemade lentil soup, or 2 (19-ounce) cans
1 bunch fresh fennel leaves, chopped (optional)
1/2 pound rice, cooked
Toasted Bread Crumbs (Page 52)
Grated Romano cheese

Ann Explains...

Just as it is traditional in our family to prepare Pasta con le Sarde on St. Joseph's Day, another Sicilian cook, Grace Licata, always served Pasta di San Giuseppe. That tradition is carried on today by her daughter, Tena Amico. This recipe was originally prepared using about a dozen very tiny artichokes, the narrow, pointed type. These grow abundantly in Sicily in the spring. They are picked young and are very sweet. These "baby" artichokes are rarely available in our markets, but if you can find them, they are preferable for this dish.

Cook the cauliflower or broccoli in boiling salted water. Drain well and sauté in olive oil with 1 clove of garlic. Set aside.

Remove the leaves and chokes from the artichokes, discard them, and slice the hearts thinly. Place them in a saucepan with water and some lemon juice and soak for 10 minutes. Heat the water and cook the sliced artichoke hearts for 5 minutes. Drain well, pat dry and sauté in olive oil with the other clove of garlic. Sprinkle with salt and set aside.

Boil pasta in a generous amount of salted water. Meanwhile, heat the lentil soup with the optional fennel leaves. When heated through, add rice.

Drain the spaghetti, saving at least 1 cup of the cooking water. Arrange the spaghetti on a platter and top with the lentil-and-rice mixture. Cover with the sautéed cauliflower or broccoli and artichoke hearts. Sprinkle with some of the bread crumbs and grated Romano cheese. If too dry, a little of the reserved spaghetti water and some olive oil may be added to each serving. Pass the bread crumbs and grated cheese at the table.

Vermicelli con le Acciughe
Vermicelli with Anchovy Sauce

1/4 cup olive oil
1 medium onion, diced
1 large clove garlic, minced
1 (2-ounce) can anchovies in olive oil
1 (1-pound) can plum tomatoes
1 (6-ounce) can tomato paste
1 tomato paste can water
1/4 teaspoon oregano
1/4 teaspoon basil, or 2 or 3 fresh leaves, chopped
1 teaspoon sugar (optional)
Salt and pepper to taste
1 pound vermicelli

Heat the oil in a saucepan and add the onion. Cook over medium heat stirring until golden, then add the garlic and cook another 1 or 2 minutes. Now add the anchovies and their oil; continue cooking slowly while stirring until the anchovies dissolve.

Crush the plum tomatoes in a bowl, add to the pan and cook 5 minutes. Add the tomato paste, water and seasonings, mix well and cook for 30 to 45 minutes, or until the consistency is thick enough for serving. Check the seasoning midway into cooking.

Cook pasta *al dente* and drain well. Return to the pan, add a small portion of the sauce to the pasta and combine. Arrange on a serving platter or individual dishes and cover with additional sauce.

Variation (Anchovy, Black Olive and Caper Sauce)

Midway into cooking the sauce, add 12 cured black Italian olives, cut in half, and 2 tablespoons capers, rinsed and well drained.

Ann Explains…
When making sauces with canned tomato products, I have a habit of using the empty can to measure any added liquid. This allows me to use up any last bit of sauce or paste that may still be clinging to the can. I guess my grandmother's lesson about never wasting anything is deeply ingrained in me.

Spaghetti con Salsa di Calamari
Spaghetti with Squid Sauce

Ann's Tips...

Do not be intimidated by the idea of cleaning squid. It is not difficult. Place the squid in a pan of cold water. It is best to work at the sink with a colander and cutting board nearby. Hold the squid in one hand and gently pull the tentacles away from the main body or sac. Set the sac aside. Cut the tentacles above the eyes. Reserve the tentacles and discard everything else from the eyes down.

To clean the sac, rub the skin off under running water. It will come off very easily. Remove and discard all the contents of the sac, including the feathery bone. Tear off the fins to include in your recipe. These are tender morsels and should not be wasted.

Further preparation of the sac depends on the recipe. It is a natural vehicle for stuffing, in which case it is left in one piece. If you will be frying it or using it in a salad, slice it into rings. For inclusion in a pasta sauce such as this, I like to cut it into pieces. Cut the body open, lay it flat and cut in 2-inch squares. Add the pieces to your sauce along with the reserved fins and tentacles.

1-1/2 pounds calamari

3 tablespoons olive oil

1 medium onion, diced

1 large clove garlic, minced

2 or 3 anchovy fillets (optional)

1 (28-ounce) can plum tomatoes

1 (6-ounce) can tomato paste

1 tomato paste can water

2 teaspoons salt, or less, to taste

1 teaspoon sugar

1/2 teaspoon basil

1/4 teaspoon oregano

1/2 teaspoon pepper

1 tablespoon chopped fresh parsley, or 2 teaspoons dried

1 small bay leaf

1/4 cup dry white wine (optional)

1 pound spaghetti or linguine, cooked

Toasted Bread Crumbs (Page 52)

Clean the squid and set it aside. Heat the oil in a saucepan, add the diced onion and cook over a medium heat for a few minutes. Add the garlic and cook an additional 3 minutes. Add the optional anchovies and stir while cooking with a wooden spoon until anchovies are dissolved. If using anchovies, be sure to adjust the salt.

Remove 5 or 6 tomatoes from the can, chop them and set aside. Place the balance of the tomatoes and the liquid in a blender and blend for 30 seconds. Add this to the onion-garlic mixture in the pan together with the tomato paste and water. Stir and cook for 15 minutes.

Add the seasonings, reserved chopped tomatoes and optional wine and simmer for 1 hour. Add the squid and cook gently until they are tender. Start checking after 25 minutes.

Serve over pasta and sprinkle with bread crumbs.

Riso alla Anna
Rice, Ann's Style

1 stick butter, divided

1 large or 2 medium onions, minced

1/2 pound fresh mushrooms, chopped

2 cups rice

4 cups water, or 3 cups water plus 1 cup white wine

4 beef bouillon cubes

1/2 teaspoon thyme

1/2 teaspoon garlic salt

1/2 to 3/4 cup grated Romano or Parmesan cheese

24 pitted ripe olives, halved or quartered

Pepper

1/2 cup minced fresh parsley

Melt 6 tablespoons of the butter and add the onion. Sauté for about 5 minutes. Add the mushrooms and continue cooking until the mixture begins to brown. Remove from the pan and set aside.

In the same pan, add the remaining 2 tablespoons of butter together with the rice and stir while cooking for about 2 minutes. Add 1 cup of water, cover and cook over a low heat, until the water is absorbed. Add the balance of the water and optional wine together with the bouillon cubes, thyme and garlic salt.

Bring the mixture to a boil again, cover, reduce to a simmer and cook until all the liquid is absorbed. Stir in the onion-mushroom mixture, cheese, olives and pepper. Continue cooking for 3 to 5 minutes. Stir in parsley and serve hot.

Variation One

Add 3 strips of lean bacon, minced, to the butter when sautéing onions and mushrooms.

Variation Two

Substitute chicken bouillon cubes for beef when serving chicken dishes. (Continued on following page.)

Ann Explains...

When you have served potatoes too often and are looking for a change of pace, this recipe will serve you well as a side dish. You'll find yourself turning to it often because of the variety of ways it can be served. Using wine as part of the cooking liquid will make this a more flavorful dish.

Rice, Ann's Style

Variation Three

Substitute sliced pimento-stuffed olives for the ripe olives.

Variation Four

Substitute chicken or vegetable bouillon cubes for beef. Add 2 cans of tuna or shrimp together with 1 package of cooked frozen peas or chopped broccoli. Put the contents into a buttered casserole, sprinkle with 2 or 3 tablespoons of seasoned bread crumbs and paprika, dot with butter, and bake in a preheated 350-degree oven until bubbly hot. Baking time will vary depending on whether it is baked while the mixture is hot or if it has been prepared in advance for baking later.

Variation Five

Omit the olives and dissolve 1/8 teaspoon or more of Spanish saffron into 1 cup of chicken bouillon before adding it to the rice. Using part white wine for the liquid is especially good with this variation. Serve with veal stew or chicken.

Variation Six

To the basic recipe add 1 pound sautéed ground beef seasoned with a little salt, basil and oregano. Olives may be omitted. This is good for use in stuffing peppers.

Italian Proverb

"A tavola, non si invecchia."

•

(At the table, no one grows older.)

•

Arancini con Tonno
Tuna-Stuffed Rice Balls

1 cup rice, cooked in two cups of salted water
3 tablespoons butter
1/2 cup grated Romano or Parmesan cheese
2 egg yolks plus 1 whole egg
1 can Italian tuna packed in olive oil, well drained
2 egg whites plus 1 whole egg
Flour
1-1/2 cups bread crumbs
Tomato Sauce and Peas (optional) (recipe follows)

Cook the rice, then add the butter, grated cheese, egg yolks and whole egg. Combine well and spread, about 1/2-inch deep, on a wet platter or cookie sheet. Cover with wax paper and cool.

Divide the rice into 10 portions. Using wet hands, put a portion of the rice on one hand and make a dent in the center. Put a small portion of the drained tuna on the rice and form it into a ball. Place on wax paper and continue until all are done.

Combine the 2 egg whites and 1 whole egg with a little salt. Roll the rice balls in flour and when all are done dip in the egg mixture and then in the bread crumbs. Let them stand 30 minutes.

Brown them in hot olive oil turning gently with 2 forks. When brown, place on paper towels. Before serving, place them in a preheated 325-degree oven for 20 minutes, or until heated through.

Can be eaten as they are or served with Tomato Sauce and Peas. *(Continued on following page.)*

Ann's Tips...

The word arancini means "little oranges," which is a reference to the size and color of the finished rice balls. This is a variation in which I substitute tuna for the meat filling my mother used in her traditional Arancini alla Siciliana. These were always found heaped high on platters at weddings, baptisms and other celebrations.

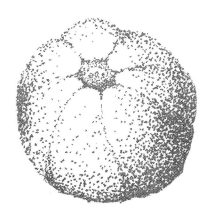

Tuna-Stuffed Rice Balls

Tomato Sauce and Peas

1/4 cup olive oil
1 medium onion, diced
1 small clove garlic, minced
1/2 cup each: chopped celery, minced carrot
1/4 green pepper, diced
1 (16-ounce) can tomato sauce
1/2 cup water
1 teaspoon sugar
Salt and pepper to taste
1/4 teaspoon each: basil, oregano
2 teaspoons chopped fresh parsley
1 cup cooked peas, well drained

Ann Explains...

Today, arancini are often offered as an appetizer course, but I also like to include this meatless version on my Lenten menus teamed with a tomato sauce prepared with peas.

Heat the oil in a saucepan and add the onion. Cook over a medium heat for 2 minutes. Add the garlic, celery, carrots and green pepper and continue to cook until the vegetables take on a little color. Add the tomato sauce, water and seasonings. Cook over a low heat for 20 to 30 minutes. Add the peas and heat through. Spoon a little sauce over each rice ball.

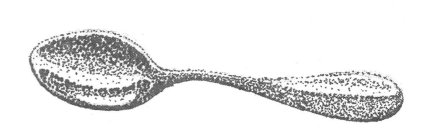

Carne, Pollo e Pesce
Meat, Chicken and Fish

Manzo Brasato
Beef Pot Roast

3 to 4 pounds eye of round roast
Salt
Pepper
Flour
Paprika
2 tablespoons olive oil
1 tablespoon butter
1 large onion, chopped
1 large or 2 medium carrots, shredded
2 large celery ribs, diced
1 large clove garlic, cut up
1 (16-ounce) can tomatoes, cut up
Red wine
1 teaspoon salt
1/4 teaspoon pepper
1 bay leaf
1/8 teaspoon rosemary
Dash ground cloves

Ann's Tips...

When braising meat, first brown it slowly on all sides to seal in the juices. Cover it tightly and simmer at a very low heat until it is fork-tender. The liquid should never boil, as this will toughen the meat.

Wash the roast, pat it dry and sprinkle it lightly with salt, pepper, flour and paprika. Heat the olive oil and butter in a Dutch oven or roasting pan with a tight-fitting lid. Brown the meat on all sides in the oil and butter. Remove and set aside.

Add the onion, carrots, celery and garlic to the pan. Drain the liquid from the canned tomatoes into a large measuring cup and add enough red wine to make 2 cups of liquid. Add the cut-up tomatoes to the vegetables and place the meat on top. Add the measured liquid and the remaining seasonings.

Bake in a preheated 325-degree oven for 2-1/2 to 3 hours, or until very tender. (You may also cook on the stove top over very low heat for same length of time). When tender, set the meat aside. Remove the bay leaf. Put the vegetables and pan juices through a food mill or puree them in a blender in 2 batches. Serve with the sliced meat.

Bistecche alla Siciliana
Beefsteaks, Sicilian-Style

1/3 cup olive oil
1 large or 2 small cloves garlic
6 small sirloin-tip steaks or filets of beef, 1/2-inch thick
1-1/2 cups seeded chopped ripe tomatoes
24 pitted black olives
1 small celery rib, thinly sliced
1/2 cup thinly sliced green pepper
2 tablespoons capers
1 teaspoon sugar
1 tablespoon wine vinegar
Salt and pepper to taste
Oregano

Sicilian Proverb

"Carni metti carni,
pisci ti nutrisci."

•

*(Meat makes you strong,
fish nurtures you.)*

•

Heat the oil in a heavy skillet and add the garlic. Cook the garlic while crushing it with a fork until it is golden. Remove it from the pan and discard. Add the steaks and cook them over a high heat for 2 or 3 minutes on each side.

Add the tomatoes, olives, celery, green pepper and capers to the pan. Mix the sugar into the vinegar and stir into the sauce. Season with salt and pepper and sprinkle with oregano. (If you are fortunate to have some growing fresh, that is best.) Cook for a few minutes to combine flavors and serve at once.

Farsumagru (Falso Magro)
Meat Roll, Sicilian-Style

1/3 cup bread crumbs

1 small clove garlic, minced

1 teaspoon chopped fresh parsley

1/4 teaspoon oregano

1/4 teaspoon basil

3/4 teaspoon salt

1/8 teaspoon pepper

1/4 cup water, wine or tomato juice

1 egg

1 pound ground veal or beef

1 round steak, 1-1/2 pounds, sliced 1/4-inch thick

8 thin slices boiled ham or prosciutto

1-1/2 cups shredded provolone or caciocavallo cheese

1/4 cup olive oil

Ann Explains...

Apparently this meat roll was used in lieu of a piece of tender meat suitable for roasting. "Farsu" means false and "magru" means lean, poor or meager in the Sicilian language. The implication is that, because of all of its rich fixings and dressing up, this dish is anything but meager.

Combine the bread crumbs, garlic, parsley, oregano, basil, salt and pepper. Add water, wine or tomato juice, and egg. Gradually add the ground meat and combine into a smooth mixture.

Place the round steak on wax paper, remove the excess fat and the round bone. Bring all the openings together. On this, spread the ground meat mixture. This is made easier by placing another piece of wax paper over the ground meat and pressing from the center out to within 1/2 inch from the edge.

Place the ham slices on the narrow end of the steak and spread the cheese over it. Place the narrow end of the steak closest to you and start rolling the meat as tightly as possible, folding in the edges as you roll. Tie the roll in 3 or 4 places with clean string.

Heat the oil in a heavy skillet or pan and brown the meat on all sides. Place the browned meat roll into a baking dish and cover with the following:

Meat Roll, Sicilian-Style

Tomato/Wine Sauce

1/3 cup dry white or red wine
1/3 cup water
Salt and pepper to taste
1 (8-ounce) can tomato sauce
1/4 teaspoon onion salt
1/2 teaspoon garlic salt
1/8 teaspoon pepper
1 teaspoon dried parsley, or 1 tablespoon chopped fresh
1 tablespoon grated Romano or Parmesan cheese
3 slices mozzarella cheese

Into the skillet where the meat was browned add the wine and water and bring to a boil. Scrape off any brown particles that may be in the pan and pour the hot liquid over the meat roll; season lightly with salt and pepper. Mix the tomato sauce with the next 5 ingredients, and pour over the meat roll.

Cover and place in a preheated 300-degree oven. Bake for 1-1/4 hours. Remove the cover. Cut the 3 cheese slices in half diagonally. Place them in an overlapping pattern on the meat. Return to the oven for 5 to 7 minutes, or until the cheese begins to melt.

Serve on a hot platter surrounded by the pan juices. Farsumagru will be easier to slice if allowed to rest for 15 to 20 minutes after it is removed from the oven.

Italian Proverb

"In un solo tegame
non c'è posto,
per cucinare lesso
e arrosto."

•

(There isn't room enough in one pot to boil meat and roast it.)

•

Farsumagru cu Muddica
Sicilian Meat Roll with Bread Crumbs

1-1/2 to 2 pounds round steak
2 cups bread crumbs
2 small cloves garlic
1/2 cup grated Romano or Parmesan cheese
3/4 teaspoon salt
1/2 teaspoon pepper
1/2 teaspoon oregano
1 teaspoon basil
2 tablespoons chopped fresh parsley
3/4 cup olive oil, divided
4 strips lean bacon
6 green onions
6 to 8 (1/4-inch-by-1-1/2-inch) strips caciocavallo or provolone cheese,
2 hard-boiled eggs, quartered (optional)
Tomato/Wine Sauce (Page 95)

Lay out the round steak and remove the excess fat and bone. Bring all the openings as close together as possible. Combine the next 8 ingredients and stir in 1/2 cup olive oil. Spread the crumb mixture over the entire surface of the meat.

At the narrow end, place the bacon slices side by side in 2 rows. On top of this, place the onions with about an inch or so of green attached. Next line up the cheese strips and optional eggs. Placing the narrow end nearest to you, roll the meat securely, folding in the ends as you go. Tie in 3 or 4 places with clean string. Heat 1/4 cup of oil in a large heavy skillet and brown on all sides. Transfer to a baking dish.

Proceed as directed from the Tomato/Wine Sauce onward in previous recipe, eliminating the mozzarella cheese if desired.

Carne "Amordicata" Arrostita
Breaded Beefsteak Cooked on an Open Grill

5 T-bone steaks, 1/2- to 3/4-inch thick
1/4 to 1 teaspoon Worcestershire sauce (optional)
1/3 cup olive oil
2 cups bread crumbs
1/3 cup grated Romano cheese
1/4 cup minced fresh parsley, or 2 teaspoons dried
4 large fresh basil leaves, minced, or 1 teaspoon dried
1/2 teaspoon oregano
1 teaspoon salt
1/2 teaspoon pepper

Ann's Tips...

If you are not a purist and are willing to try this method of cooking a steak, you are in for a treat. The seasoned bread crumbs capture the juices of the steak as it broils over the hot coals, resulting in a delicious, crunchy taste experience. The choice of steak is yours, but this works best with a good cut of meat.

Remove any excess fat from the meat and make cuts every inch or so around the edge of the steaks so that the meat remains flat while cooking. Mix optional Worcestershire sauce with the oil. Using a pastry brush, paint each steak with the oil mixture on both sides and stack the steaks.

Mix the bread crumbs with all the remaining ingredients and place the mixture on a flat dish or wax paper. Dip each steak in the crumbs on both sides, gently pressing the mixture onto the steak. Let them set on wax paper for 15 minutes.

Meanwhile, prepare a charcoal fire. Place the rack 5 or 6 inches from the coals and, when they are hot, place the steaks on the rack, turning them 2 or 3 times. It is important that the meat is not too close to the fire or the crumbs will burn. When the steaks are browned on both sides they should be served immediately.

Braciole di Manzo con Vino e Funghi
Beef Rolls with Mushrooms and Wine Sauce

Bread Dressing (recipe follows)
8 to 10 very thin slices sirloin-tip steaks
1/2 cup flour
1/2 teaspoon salt
1/4 cup olive oil plus 1 tablespoon butter
1 (8-ounce) can sliced mushrooms
Onion salt
Garlic salt
Basil
Oregano
Pepper
1 cup Burgundy, or other red table wine

Ann's Tips...
Italian cooks from many regions prepare Braciole in tomato sauce to serve with their pasta. In this version, I brown them and then bake them with wine, beef bouillon and mushrooms. This recipe goes well with Riso alla Anna (Page 87) or fluffy mashed potatoes.

Prepare the Bread Dressing. On wax paper, lay out the steaks and spread some bread dressing over each one. Roll the meat and secure with wooden picks.

Combine the flour and salt. Roll the beef rolls in the flour and shake off the excess. Heat the oil and butter in a skillet and brown the rolls on all sides. Place the beef rolls in a casserole or baking pan.

Drain the mushrooms and reserve the liquid. Add the mushrooms to the skillet and sauté. Distribute the mushrooms over the beef rolls and sprinkle the meat lightly with onion and garlic salts, basil, oregano, and pepper.

Add the wine to the skillet together with the reserved mushroom liquid. Heat and loosen any brown crusty particles from the pan. Add this hot mixture to the casserole, cover and bake in a 325-degree oven for 1 hour. Add a small amount of hot water from time to time if necessary.

Cook's Note: This may be assembled in advance, and refrigerated. An hour before baking, remove from the refrigerator and bake as above.

Beef Rolls with Mushrooms and Wine Sauce

Bread Dressing

1/4 cup olive oil
1 small onion, diced
1 small clove garlic, through a press or minced
1 cup bread crumbs
1/3 cup grated Romano or Parmesan cheese
1/2 teaspoon salt
1/4 teaspoon pepper
1/4 teaspoon oregano
1/2 teaspoon basil
1 tablespoon chopped fresh parsley

Heat the oil and gently cook the onion until it is soft and golden. Add the garlic and cook another minute or so and remove from the heat. Combine the bread crumbs, grated cheese and seasonings in a bowl. Add to the contents in the pan and combine until all the crumbs are coated with oil.

Italian Proverb

"Pane all'usanza antica,
prima la crosta poi
la mollica."

•

*(Bread the old-fashioned
way: first the crust
and then the crumbs.)*

•

From Ann's Kitchen

Stufato di Manzo
Beef Stew

1/2 cup flour
Salt
Pepper
1-1/2 to 2 pounds boneless beef stew
1/3 cup olive oil
1 medium onion, minced
1 clove garlic, through a press
2 whole allspice (optional)
1 bay leaf
1/2 teaspoon Worcestershire sauce
1 beef bouillon cube
Water
1/2 cup dry white or red wine
1 cup cut-up tomatoes
1/2 teaspoon oregano
1/2 teaspoon basil
1 tablespoon minced fresh parsley, or 1 teaspoon dried
6 medium potatoes, pared and quartered
6 small whole onions
3 or 4 medium carrots, pared and cut in thirds
1 can best quality peas
1 tablespoon butter (optional)
Additional fresh parsley, minced (optional)
Onion powder (optional)
Paprika, parsley for garnish (optional)

Ann Explains...

There are certain hearty "comfort foods" that satisfy the soul. We make them often because our families look forward to coming home to them.

Put the flour in a clean paper or plastic bag with 1/2 teaspoon of salt and 1/8 teaspoon of pepper. Shake well and add a few pieces of meat at a time. Shake meat to coat well on all sides and remove to a colander. Continue until all meat is coated then shake meat in the colander to remove excess flour.

Beef Stew

Heat the oil in a Dutch oven and add enough meat to make only one layer; do not crowd. Cook over a medium-high heat, turning to brown on all sides. Remove the browned meat from the pan and set aside. Add any remaining pieces and cook until all are browned.

Add the onion and garlic to the oil remaining in the pan and cook gently until the onion is transparent and turns a nice golden color. Return the meat to the pan and add 1 teaspoon of salt, 1/4 teaspoon of pepper, optional allspice, bay leaf, Worcestershire sauce, bouillon cube, 1 cup hot water and wine. Place the tomatoes directly on the meat and sprinkle the oregano, basil and parsley over them.

Cover the pan and, when it begins to boil, reduce to the lowest simmer and cook for about 1-1/2 hours. Check every half hour to see if additional water needs to be added.

Now move all the meat to the center of the pan and, around the sides, add the potatoes, onions and carrots. Be sure there is enough liquid to come at least 3/4 way up around the vegetables. Season them lightly with salt and pepper, cover and cook for an additional 45 minutes to 1 hour, or until the meat and vegetables are cooked through.

In a small saucepan, place the peas and half of their juice and bring to a boil. Drain off most of the liquid and season with butter, onion powder and parsley if desired. Keep over low heat until ready to use.

On a large hot platter arrange the potatoes, carrots, peas and onions around the edge to form a circle. Put all the meat in the center and pour on some of the brown gravy. Sprinkle the platter lightly with paprika and parsley if desired. Serve at once with hot crusty bread and pass the rest of the gravy.

Menu Suggestion

An Autumn Dinner

•

Insalata di Arance alla Siciliana

•

Stufato di Manzo

•

Pane e Burro

•

Bocconcini Dolci

•

Polpette e Peperoni con Salsa di Pomodoro
Meatballs and Peppers in Tomato Sauce

1 recipe Polpette (Page 72)
2 tablespoons olive oil, plus additional for browning
1 small onion, chopped
1 clove garlic, minced
2 (1-pound) cans and 1 (8-ounce) can tomato sauce
2 teaspoons basil
1 teaspoon oregano
1 teaspoon sugar
1/8 teaspoon pepper
1-1/2 teaspoons grated Romano cheese
Salt to taste
2 pounds green peppers, sliced

Prepare the Polpette mixture and form into 1-1/2-inch balls. Brown them in a small amount of oil and set aside.

In a 3-quart pot, heat the 2 tablespoons olive oil and sauté the onion. When it is almost golden, add the minced garlic and cook a few more minutes. Add the tomato sauce and remaining seasonings and cook for 10 to 15 minutes.

Lower the meatballs and peppers into the sauce and simmer gently for 30 to 40 minutes, or until the flavors are blended and the peppers are cooked.

Arrosto di Vitello
Veal Roast

1 veal rump roast, 3-1/2 to 4 pounds
1 small onion, sliced
1 large rib celery with leaves, cut into strips
1 medium carrot, cut into strips
2 or 3 sprigs fresh parsley
2 fresh basil leaves, minced
2 or 3 fresh mint leaves
Olive or vegetable oil
1-1/2 cups water, divided
1 clove garlic, cut
Salt and pepper
1 chicken or beef bouillon cube

Select a good cut of veal, either with the bone or without. Wash and pat dry. Select a shallow roasting pan that is large enough to hold the roast, but no larger. Place the vegetables and herbs in the center of the pan to make a bed for the roast. Pour 1/2 cup of oil over the vegetables and 1/2 cup of water around them. Rub the meat on all sides with garlic and a little oil. Season with salt and pepper.

Place the meat on the vegetables and put the pan in a preheated 325-degree oven for 30 minutes per pound, or until a meat thermometer registers 170 degrees. As the meat begins to brown, take drippings from the bottom of the pan and pour them over the roast. Watch carefully. To avoid drying out continue to add a little hot water from time to time as needed.

When done remove the roast to a hot platter and keep it covered. Put all the vegetables and pan juices in a strainer or food mill and press out all the juices as well as the vegetable pulp. Be sure to scrape off all brown particles adhering to the pan and add to the mixture.

Dissolve a bouillon cube in 1 cup of boiling water. Add to it the strained pan juices and cook gently for about 5 minutes to combine the flavors. Thicken with a little flour if desired.

Cook's Note: Roast may be sliced at the table or sliced and arranged on a hot platter with some of the gravy spooned over the slices. Any additional gravy may be passed around in a bowl.

Ann's Tips...
When preparing a roast, plan to have it done 15 to 20 minutes before serving to allow time for making the gravy. The roast will also be easier to carve if it has "rested."

Arrosto di Vitello alla Siciliana
Roast Leg of Veal, Sicilian-Style

1 leg of veal, 7 to 8 pounds

1 teaspoon salt

1/2 teaspoon pepper

1/2 teaspoon oregano

1/2 teaspoon dried basil, or 2 teaspoons chopped fresh

1/2 teaspoon dried mint, or 2 teaspoons chopped fresh

1 small onion, minced

1 clove garlic, through a press or minced

3 slices bacon, minced

1 teaspoon Worcestershire sauce (optional)

Olive oil

Salt and pepper to taste

1 (8-ounce) can sliced mushrooms

1 cup Sauterne wine

Wipe the leg of veal with a damp cloth. Make 1-inch slits on all sides of the veal. Combine the next 8 ingredients and fill each slit with the mixture. Mix the Worcestershire sauce if desired with a small amount of olive oil and rub the entire roast with it. Sprinkle with salt and pepper and place it in an uncovered roasting pan.

Put into a preheated 325-degree oven and cook for 25 to 30 minutes per pound, or until a meat thermometer registers 170 degrees. When the meat begins to brown and the pan juices begin to form a crust at the bottom of the pan, add the mushrooms. After 20 minutes, add the wine. Watch closely and, if the wine evaporates too much, add some hot water, a half cup at a time. Serve with the pan juices or, if desired, add enough water to make 2 cups of liquid and thicken with 2 tablespoons of cornstarch or flour.

Cotolette di Vitello
Breaded Veal Cutlets

2 pounds veal cutlets
2 tablespoons water
Salt and pepper
2 large eggs
Romano or Parmesan cheese, grated (optional)
2 cups Seasoned Bread Crumbs (Page 52)
1/2 cup olive and corn oils, combined

Pound the veal cutlets to make thin even pieces. Add the water, salt and pepper to the eggs and beat well. If more cheese flavor is desired than that imparted by the bread crumbs, you may add an additional tablespoonful or 2 to the beaten eggs.

Pass each cutlet through the bread crumbs, dip it into the egg mixture and drain off the excess, then dip it into the bread crumbs. Place the cutlets on wax paper, letting them stand for about 20 minutes. Turn and let stand another 10 minutes.

Heat the oil in a heavy skillet until hot. If you prefer, you may use part olive oil and part butter. Adjust to a medium heat and put in the veal cutlets. Do not crowd. Cook to a golden brown on one side, then turn to cook the second side. Place on paper towels. Continue with additional meat until all the cutlets are cooked.

To keep warm, put cutlets in a shallow baking dish and set in a preheated 250-degree oven. If necessary, cover with aluminum foil. Remove the foil 5 minutes before serving.

Ann Explains...

One of the reasons veal is so popular in Italy is that the quality is generally better than what we can purchase here. The best veal is milk-fed and almost white in color. The pinker veal in our markets can be quite good for some dishes, such as these breaded cutlets. Use a meat mallet to pound the veal between pieces of wax paper until the meat is as thin as you wish.

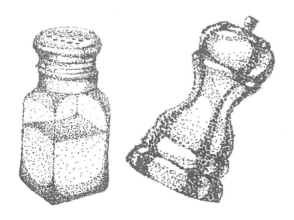

Cotolette di Vitello alla Sorrentino
Veal Cutlets, Sorrentino-Style

1 cup Marinara Sauce (recipe follows)
1 medium eggplant
3/4 cup flour
Salt and pepper
8 veal cutlets, 1/4-inch thick (4-ounces each)
2 eggs, divided
1 tablespoon water
3/4 cup dry bread crumbs
5 tablespoons grated Romano cheese, divided
5 teaspoons minced fresh parsley, divided
1 small clove garlic, minced
1 cup ricotta cheese, very well drained
1/2 cup olive oil
1/2 cup corn oil
4 slices mozzarella cheese

Prepare Marinara Sauce and set aside.

Peel the eggplant and cut it into lengthwise slices. Sprinkle the slices with salt and place on a plate in layers between sheets of paper towel. Put a heavy bowl or something else of weight on top and allow to rest for 1/2 hour. Pat dry with paper towels.

Season the flour with 1/2 teaspoon of salt and 1/4 teaspoon of pepper. Flour the cutlets, shaking off any excess flour. Set aside.

Beat 1 egg with 1 tablespoon of water. Season the bread crumbs with 3 tablespoons of grated cheese, 3 teaspoons of parsley, garlic, and salt and pepper to taste. Mix well. Dip the cutlets in the egg wash, drain the excess and dip into the seasoned bread crumbs. Press the crumbs firmly into the cutlets and place them on wax paper to dry for about 30 minutes, turning once.

Whip up the ricotta with the remaining 2 tablespoons of grated cheese, 2 teaspoons of parsley, a little salt and pepper, and the remaining egg. Set in the refrigerator until needed.

Veal Cutlets, Sorrentino-Style

Heat 1/4 cup each of the oils in a broad Teflon-coated frying pan. When hot, cook the cutlets until they are a golden brown color. Set aside. Add the remaining oil and heat until hot. Dip the eggplant slices in the remaining flour, shake off any excess and fry until golden. Place on paper towels.

Place the cutlets in a baking dish or pan that holds them without crowding. On each cutlet, place 2 tablespoons of the ricotta mixture and cover with 1 slice of eggplant. Spoon the sauce on each eggplant slice. Cut the mozzarella cheese slices in half. Place 1 piece on each cutlet. Bake in a preheated 350-degree oven until the cutlets are heated through and the cheese is melted.

Marinara Sauce

1/4 cup olive oil
1 clove garlic, minced
1 (15-ounce) can tomatoes, pureed in a blender or sieved
3/4 teaspoon salt
1/2 teaspoon oregano
1/4 teaspoon basil
1 teaspoon chopped fresh parsley
Pepper

Heat the oil in a saucepan and gently cook the garlic until it starts to turn golden brown. Watch closely; do not burn. Add the tomatoes and seasonings. Cook rapidly, uncovered, until the liquid is condensed and the sauce thickens. Stir occasionally to keep it from sticking.

Italian Proverb

"A pancia piena
si ragiona meglio."

•

*(With a full stomach,
you can think straight.)*

•

Spezzatino di Vitello con lo Zafferano
Saffron Veal Stew

Ann Explains...

When I was growing up, my mother prepared many delicious veal dishes that still bring back fond memories. In addition to this recipe, there were breaded veal cutlets (a favorite of many Italians), Sunday veal roast and many tasty veal casseroles. As a young married woman, I followed my mother's cooking style closely, serving my family those same dishes often. Today, not only is veal expensive, it is difficult to buy in the quantity and cut desired. On the rare occasion that I do find what I want, I spend the extra money and treat my family. What I find myself doing more and more, however, is substituting chicken breast for veal. Admitting at the start that chicken does not taste exactly like veal, I still find it to be delicious in its own right. And sometimes, it's the only way to satisfy the yearning for those old-time flavors.

1/4 cup olive oil
4 tablespoons butter, divided
1-1/2 pounds leg of veal, cut into 1-1/2- to 2-inch cubes
1 small onion, minced
2 cloves garlic, minced
3 tablespoons chopped fresh parsley
1/2 pound sliced fresh mushrooms (optional)
1/2 cup dry white wine
Hot water
1 beef bouillon cube
Salt and pepper
1/8 teaspoon saffron powder
3 medium carrots, cut into strips
1 (10-ounce) package frozen peas
1/2 teaspoon sugar (optional)
Onion salt and pepper
1/2 pound linguine, or 1 cup uncooked rice
3 tablespoons grated Romano or Parmesan cheese
Fresh parsley
Paprika

In a Dutch oven, heat the oil then add 1 tablespoon of the butter. Over a medium-high heat brown the meat on all sides. Push the meat to one side, add the onion and cook about 1 minute while stirring. Add the garlic and continue cooking until the onion begins to take on some color. Be careful that the meat does not scorch. Add the parsley and optional mushrooms and stir for another 3 minutes or so. Add the wine and enough hot water to scarcely cover. Stir in the bouillon cube, salt and pepper, and saffron. Bring to a boil, turn down to a simmer, cover and cook for about 1 hour.

Cut the carrots into thirds, then each third in half, then each half into 2 or 3 strips each. Push the meat to one side and add the carrots to one section of the pan. Cover the pan and cook for another 30 to 35 minutes, or until the meat and carrots are cooked. If necessary, add a little hot water from time to time to keep the meat covered.

Prepare the frozen peas according to the package directions. Season with optional sugar, onion salt and pepper. Set aside and keep warm.

Cook linguine according to the package directions. Drain the pasta well and put back into the pot. Add remaining 3 tablespoons of butter and grated cheese, and toss.

Place the linguine in the center of a hot platter and surround with sections of the veal, carrots and peas. If desired, liquid in the pan may be thickened with 1 or 2 teaspoons of flour. Spoon over all. Sprinkle with additional grated cheese, parsley and paprika.

To serve with rice, prepare the rice according to the package directions, using 1 chicken bouillon cube for each cup of water and omitting the salt. Season and serve as indicated above. This dish is also good with Riso alla Anna, Variation 5 (Page 88).

Ann's Tips...

With this dish, I have had luck substituting the veal with small, thin escallops of chicken breast, and reducing the cooking time.

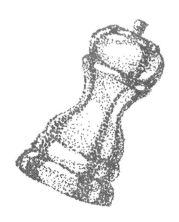

Fette di Vitello alla Sodaro
Layered Sliced Veal, Sodaro-Style

2-1/2 pounds veal, thinly sliced as for cutlets, 5-1/2- to 6-inches long
1/4 cup olive oil
Bread Dressing (Page 99)
Onion salt, Garlic salt, Pepper, Basil, Oregano
1/2 pound sliced fresh mushrooms, or 1 (4-ounce) can
Butter
1/2 cup dry white wine (optional)

Ann Explains…
This is another dish based on my childhood memories of family specialties. An alternate way to prepare this recipe is to divide the bread dressing equally on the individual slices of veal and roll them to make Bracioline di Vitello con Vino e Funghi.

To prepare this dish you will need an even number of pieces of meat, each piece having a second slice of equal proportion to serve as a top layer. To arrange the slices, place half of the total number on a sheet of wax paper, then cover each piece with a second slice, trying to match them as closely as possible.

You have now established a pattern for your baking pan. Select a baking pan large enough to hold all the meat in the pattern arranged. Pour half of the oil in and spread to cover the surface of the pan. Now, using the pattern laid out on the wax paper, take the top sections of the meat and lay them in the pan side by side. Do not leave space between the slices.

Prepare the bread dressing as directed. (If a thicker filling is desired, prepare 1-1/2 recipes of the mixture.) Spread bread dressing evenly over the entire surface of the meat in the pan. Take the remaining meat on the wax paper, place over the dressing in the same pattern as before. Sprinkle the surface of the meat lightly with onion and garlic salts, pepper, basil and oregano. Drizzle the remaining oil over all. Place in a preheated 350-degree oven and bake for 30 to 35 minutes, or until the meat is lightly browned.

Lightly sauté the mushrooms in butter. During the last 10 minutes of cooking, add the mushrooms and the wine to the baking pan. Also, a little water may be added to create some pan juices to serve over the meat.

When ready to serve, lift the meat from the pan using a spatula. Place on individual serving dishes and spoon a little of the pan juices over each. You will have a meat sandwich with a bread dressing filling. Delicious!

Carne, Pollo e Pesce ✱ Meat, Chicken and Fish

Agnello al Forno
Roast Lamb

Leg of lamb, 6 or more pounds
2 tablespoons minced fresh parsley
1 teaspoon oregano
2 or 3 mint leaves, minced, or 1/2 teaspoon dried
Salt and pepper to taste
Additional herbs
Worcestershire sauce
Olive oil
2 cloves garlic, slivered

Rinse the lamb and pat dry. Make slits all over the surface of the roast with the tip of a knife or the point of a meat thermometer.

Mix the parsley, oregano, mint, salt, pepper and any other herbs your family enjoys with lamb. Some possibilities are rosemary, thyme, basil and onion salt. Moisten the herb mixture with small amounts of Worcestershire sauce and olive oil. Insert pieces of slivered garlic and the herb mixture in each slit.

Roast in a preheated 400-degree oven for 15 minutes, then reduce the heat to 325 degrees and roast for 30 minutes per pound, or until the meat thermometer registers 170 to 175 degrees. Let the lamb rest for 20 minutes while making pan gravy.

Variation (Basted Leg of Lamb)

In a saucepan, prepare a basting sauce by blending the following ingredients: 1 cup of olive oil, 1 cup of white wine, 2 tablespoons of butter, 1 minced onion, 1 crushed clove of garlic, 1-1/2 teaspoons of oregano, 1 teaspoon of basil, 1 teaspoon of salt (or to taste), 1/2 teaspoon of pepper and 1/2 teaspoon of paprika.

Heat for 15 minutes to combine flavors. Omit the seasonings listed in Agnello al Forno (above), but roast the meat by the same method. After the first 45 minutes of cooking, baste the roast with the sauce every 15 minutes until done. The sauce also lends a special touch to lamb or veal chops.

Menu Suggestion

Easter Sunday Dinner

•

Calzone

•

Agnello al Forno

•

Patate Arrosto

•

Asparagi alla Parmigiana

•

Insalata di Pomodoro

•

Torta di Ricotta Siciliana alla Anna

•

Arrosto di Maiale
Roast Pork

Pork roast, 3-1/2 pounds or larger
Onion salt
Garlic salt
Pepper, freshly ground
Thyme
Fennel seeds, ground (Page 113)
1 tablespoon Worcestershire sauce (optional)
Water, 1/2 cup to start
2 level tablespoons flour
1 chicken or vegetable bouillon cube (optional)
Parsley sprigs for garnish

Wipe the roast and put it in a roasting pan. Season the meat on all sides with the onion and garlic salts, pepper, thyme and fennel seeds. Lightly pound the seasonings into the meat with your hands. If the Worcestershire sauce is used, spoon evenly over the top of the roast. Put about 1/2 cup of water in the pan around the meat.

Set in a preheated 350-degree oven and bake for 25 minutes per pound or until a meat thermometer registers 170 degrees. As it bakes, the fat will render in the water of the pan and, as the water evaporates, the drippings will begin to brown. Add a little more hot water from time to time so that the drippings remain a nice deep golden color and the fat does not burn.

When the roast is done remove the meat to a platter. Drain all but 2 tablespoons of the fat from the pan. Add flour to the pan and slowly add 2 cups of water while cooking over a low heat. Add bouillon cube if desired. When the gravy is thickened, taste to check the seasoning. Slice the roast and arrange the slices down the center of a platter. Spoon a small amount of gravy over it. Arrange oven-browned potatoes around the roast and tuck a few sprigs of parsley around platter. Serve hot.

Costolette di Maiale al Limone
Sautéed Pork Chops with Lemon Juice

6 loin or center-cut pork chops
1 clove garlic
Salt and pepper
1/2 teaspoon fennel seeds, ground
Juice of 2 lemons

Remove the excess fat from the pork chops. Put the trimmings into a skillet and place it on medium heat. When the fat begins to render, add the chops and brown with the garlic. Remove the garlic, season the chops with the salt, pepper and fennel seeds. Cover the pan and cook over a low heat until fork tender.

Remove the chops to a serving dish. Drain any fat from the skillet, add the lemon juice and a little water. Season to taste, heat to a boil and pour over the chops. Serve at once, accompanied by fried potatoes with onions and a vegetable of your choice.

Ann Explains...

Since I frequently use fennel in my cooking, I long ago purchased a small pepper mill and turned it into my "fennel mill." One or two turns of the mill impart a fennel flavor to sauces, roasts and other recipes. Grinding the fennel brings out a better flavor and it adheres to foods more easily than whole seeds.

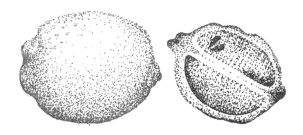

Salsiccia Casalinga
Homemade Italian Sausage

For every pound of ground pork, add:

For every pound of ground pork, add:
  1/4 cup water
  1/4 teaspoon freshly ground pepper
  1 teaspoon salt
  1 teaspoon fennel seed, whole or ground (Page 113)
  1/4 teaspoon red pepper flakes, or more, to taste

Ann's Tips...

Here is how my mother made her sausage. Some Sicilians add grated cheese or wine to their sausage, but the basic ingredients are those listed here. Regarding the amount of fat, the leanest sausage does not always taste or feel right when you bite into it. Fat provides both flavor and a good, moist texture. If making homemade sausage doesn't fit into your busy lifestyle, simply form the sausage mixture into patties, pan fry them and serve them on a Kaiser-style roll with fried peppers. This sausage mixture also makes a savory addition to poultry stuffing. Cook the seasoned meat until no pink remains and add to bread dressing along with onion, celery and other personal touches.

Select pork butt or shoulder (not too fat or too lean). Have the butcher trim any unwanted fat and grind meat large for sausage. (Some cooks prefer a regular grind.) Keep the bones to brown with your next batch of spaghetti sauce. Purchase the casings from the butcher when ordering the meat for your sausage.

Weigh the meat again after it is ground, then set aside. In a large bowl, put sufficient water and seasonings for the number of pounds of meat you are preparing. Stir to dissolve the salt, then add the meat and combine thoroughly with the seasoning. Make a small patty and brown it in a frying pan to test for seasoning. If necessary, add more of whatever you find lacking.

Place the casings into a bowl of warm water and let stand while preparing the sausage mixture. Then wash the casings in cold running water several times, letting the water run through the casings.

Carefully slide the casing onto the sausage grinder tube or sausage funnel. Make a knot at the opening of the casing, then hold onto the tube and start feeding the meat into the casing, guiding it as it goes along. Do not overfill. You can give the casing 2 or 3 twists every 5 inches to form links, or leave in one piece.

Continue until all the meat is used, then carefully prick the sausage casings in several places with a round toothpick or cake tester. This helps release fat when cooking.

Arrosto di Pollo
Roast Chicken

1 roasting chicken, 3-1/2 to 4 pounds
3 large red potatoes, or 2 large Idaho potatoes
1/3 cup vegetable or olive oil
1 to 2 teaspoons butter
1 large onion, thinly sliced
Salt and pepper to taste
1 or 2 sage leaves, crumbled (optional)
2 tablespoons chopped fresh parsley (optional)
1 tablespoon olive oil
Water or chicken broth (optional)

Wash the chicken thoroughly and set it in a colander to drain. Pare the potatoes, then slice each lengthwise into 3 slices. Cut each slice into 3 strips and slice the strips into cubes of equal size. Wash, drain well and pat the potatoes dry on paper towels.

Heat the oil in a skillet and add potatoes to the oil. Cook over a medium heat, turning frequently with a spatula, until they are golden in color. Remove to a bowl with a slotted spoon, leaving behind any excess oil.

In a small pan, melt the butter and add the onion. Cook slowly until it is transparent and golden in color. Combine the onions and potatoes and season with salt and pepper, and optional sage and parsley.

Using paper towels, pat the cavity of the washed chicken dry. Season lightly with salt and pepper, and spoon the potatoes into the cavity. The opening may be held together with skewers or by simply bringing the two legs together over the opening and tying securely with clean white string. Some of the potatoes can be put in the neck opening after seasoning with salt and pepper. Cover the opening by drawing the skin tightly over the potatoes and bringing the skin down as far as it will go. Tuck the wing tips into the back to hold the neck skin if desired.

Rub the surface of the chicken with the 1 tablespoon of olive oil and place in a small roasting pan. Roast in a preheated 350-degree oven for 1-1/4 to 1-1/2 hours, or until a meat thermometer registers 185 degrees. *(Continued on following page.)*

Ann Remembers...
My mother had an unusual way of preparing roast chicken, at least I think she did, since I have never known anyone outside of the Sodaro family to do it. Mama stuffed her chicken with fried potatoes and onions, and it was delicious.

After 45 minutes to 1 hour, skim most of the grease out of the roasting pan and add some water or chicken broth if desired. Spoon some of the pan juices over the chicken once or twice during the balance of the cooking time.

After removing from the oven, cover with foil and let stand for 10 to 15 minutes before carving. Spoon the potatoes into a bowl and serve them and the carved chicken with the pan juices.

Pollo al Forno
Oven-Baked Chicken

1 cut-up chicken, 2-3/4 to 3-1/2 pounds
1/3 cup olive oil
Salt and pepper
Onion salt
Basil
Oregano
Parsley
2 sage leaves, crumbled
Rosemary (optional)
2 cloves garlic, cut in half
Water or chicken broth (optional)
1/3 to 1/2 cup white wine

Ann Explains...

This is an easy way to prepare a cut-up chicken. The results taste somewhat like Chicken Vesuvio, a specialty of many Chicago restaurants.

Wash and pat the chicken pieces dry. Put the oil in a baking pan large enough to hold the chicken in one layer. Place the chicken in the pan, skin-side down. Sprinkle the chicken lightly with all the seasonings then turn the pieces over with the skin-side up, and repeat with the seasonings. Add the cut garlic to the baking pan.

Bake in a preheated 350-degree oven for 1-1/4 hours, or until nicely browned. Spoon the pan juices over the chicken after the first 1/2 hour. If the garlic gets too brown, remove it. During the last 15 minutes of cooking, some of the excess oil may be removed and some water or broth may be added together with the wine. Serve with oven-browned potatoes.

Pollo Arrostito con Salsa di Limone
Grilled Chicken with Lemon Sauce

2 chickens, 3 to 3-1/2 pounds, cut into serving pieces
2 recipes Condimento di Limone ed Olio (Page 26)
Garlic salt
Onion salt
Pepper, freshly ground
Paprika
Fresh parsley, chopped
Fresh mint and basil, chopped
Fresh herb stems for garnish

Wash the chicken and pat it dry with paper towels. Using a large shallow baking pan, arrange as many chicken pieces as will fit in one layer, cut side up.

Beat the lemon and oil dressing to mix well and spoon a small amount over the surface of all the chicken. Sprinkle with all of the seasonings and herbs. (If necessary substitute dried basil and mint for the fresh leaves.) Turn the chicken pieces over and repeat the seasoning process. Continue layering the remaining chicken, adding lemon dressing and seasonings.

Refrigerate the remaining dressing. Cover and refrigerate the chicken for several hours or overnight. If using aluminum foil, it is best to first cover with wax paper as the lemon juice may erode the aluminum.

Prepare a charcoal fire. Lay the chicken on the hot grill, 5 or 6 inches from coals. Discard the used marinade as it may be contaminated by the raw chicken. Cook for 40 to 45 minutes, or until the juices run clear and the meat is no longer pink.

Place the chicken on a hot platter and tuck some fresh parsley and mint or basil leaves around the edge. Pass the remaining dressing and enjoy.

Ann Remembers...

The following recipe was prepared in our home by my mother and her mother before her. It is one of the many recipes brought over from Sicily when my grandmother arrived here in 1900, and it bears a strong resemblance to the Greek way of preparing chicken. Originally the lemon-and-oil sauce was basted over the chicken with a few oregano stems, tied together, with the leaves still attached. This makes a good, stiff brush and lends a delicious flavor to the chicken. At meal time, the brush was passed around the table with the sauce. Dried oregano stems may occasionally be found in Italian or Greek specialty stores. Lacking an oregano brush, a spoon will do just fine.

Petti di Pollo
Breaded Chicken Breasts, Italian-Style

4 large chicken breasts, boned
Salt and pepper
1 large egg
1 tablespoon water or milk
1/2 cup flour
1-1/2 cups Seasoned Bread Crumbs (Page 52)
1/3 cup olive oil
2 tablespoons butter or margarine

See Page 52

Italian Proverb

"Amici e vino vogliono
essere vecchi."

•

(Friends and wine
should be old.)

•

Have a butcher split and bone 2 large whole chicken breasts. Remove any skin or visible fat before breading. Season lightly on both sides with salt and pepper. Beat egg with water or milk. Dip each piece first in flour, shaking off the excess, then in the egg mixture. Coat with bread crumbs using the palms of your hands to press in the crumbs. Place on wax paper and let rest for 10 to 15 minutes on each side.

Heat the oil and butter in a heavy skillet and brown to a golden color on both sides. The chicken breasts may be prepared in advance up until this point. Place in an oven-proof dish and bake in a preheated 300-degree oven for 20 to 30 minutes just before serving.

Petti di Pollo con Funghi e Carciofi
Chicken Breasts with Mushrooms and Artichokes

1/2 cup flour
1/4 teaspoon each: garlic salt, onion salt
1/4 teaspoon each: dried basil, oregano, parsley, pepper
6 skinless and boneless chicken breasts
1/4 cup olive oil
2 tablespoons butter
1 small onion, diced
1/4 pound fresh mushrooms, sliced
1 (10-ounce) package frozen artichokes, thawed, or 1 tall can artichoke
  hearts, well drained
3/4 cup water
1/2 cup dry white wine
1 chicken bouillon cube
Paprika

Combine the flour with the seasonings and mix well. Pound the chicken breasts between 2 sheets of wax paper to flatten slightly if desired. Roll the chicken in the seasoned flour.

Heat the olive oil and butter in a skillet and add the chicken breasts. Do not cover. When they are nicely browned, remove them from the skillet and set aside. If necessary, add more butter to the skillet and add the diced onion and sauté until soft. Add the mushrooms and artichokes and continue to cook until golden. Cook a few minutes, remove them from the pan and set aside. If using canned artichokes, they should be added after the mushrooms are completely sautéed.

Combine the water, wine and bouillon cube in the skillet and bring to a boil. Cook until the bouillon cube is dissolved. Return the chicken to the skillet and cover with the sautéed vegetables. Sprinkle them lightly with additional basil, oregano and paprika. Cover and cook on a low heat for 20 to 25 minutes adding more water if the liquid evaporates.

Oven Method: The chicken may be placed in a baking pan, topped with the vegetables, covered with aluminum foil and baked in a preheated 350-degree oven for 20 to 25 minutes, or until hot and bubbly. This recipe may be prepared in advance and baked before serving, allowing more time to bake.

Menu Suggestion

Sunday Dinner

•

Petti di Pollo con Funghi e Carciofi

•

Riso alla Anna

•

Fagiolini al Pomodoro

•

Insalata di Verdura Italiana

•

Torta di Mele alla Zia Anna

•

Fette di Tonno Fritto con Cipolle
Sliced Fresh Tuna Fried with Onions

1-1/2 pounds fresh tuna, sliced 1/4-inch thick
1/3 cup flour
1/2 teaspoon garlic salt
1/2 teaspoon each: dried basil, dried oregano
1/3 cup olive oil
1 large onion, thickly sliced
1/4 cup wine vinegar
2 tablespoons water
Salt and pepper to taste
1/2 to 1 teaspoon sugar (optional)
Fresh parsley and basil, chopped, for garnish (optional)

Ann Explains…

Throughout Italy, it is popular to serve a cold dish of fish or veal with a piquant wine-vinegar sauce. It may be served as an appetizer or, especially in the summer, as a main dish. Here is my version, featuring fresh tuna.

Cut the tuna into serving pieces. Mix the flour with the garlic salt and herbs. Dust the tuna slices in the seasoned flour. Heat the oil in a skillet (non-stick, if possible). Brown the tuna in the hot oil without crowding the pan. Place the fish on a large dish or small platter, slightly overlapping the slices.

Add the onion to the skillet and cook over moderate heat until limp and lightly browned. Add the vinegar, water, salt, pepper and optional sugar. Cook a few minutes to combine the flavors. Pour the mixture evenly over the tuna slices. Let stand a half hour and serve. If desired, sprinkle with chopped parsley and basil. This dish is very good served cold.

Pesce Spada Fritto
Fried Swordfish

2 large eggs
2 tablespoons water
1/4 cup grated Romano cheese
1 clove garlic, through a press
2 tablespoons chopped fresh flat-leaf parsley
Salt and pepper to taste
2 pounds swordfish
2 cups bread crumbs
Olive oil
Lemons, parsley for garnish

Beat the eggs with the water, cheese, garlic, parsley, and salt and pepper. For the best flavor, do not substitute with dried parsley. Dip each piece of fish in the egg/cheese mixture and then in the bread crumbs. Place the fish on wax paper and let it stand for 30 minutes, turning once. Heat the olive oil in a skillet and carefully fry the fish to a golden brown. Place the fish in a baking or jelly-roll pan and bake in a preheated 325-degree oven for 30 minutes. Serve on a platter decorated with lemon wedges and parsley.

Ann's Tips...

This is always on our table on Christmas Eve, and it is one of the most anticipated of all the foods served. If any family member was unable to be with us that night, they come through the door on Christmas Day asking, "Is there any swordfish left over?" Since swordfish is expensive and there is usually a crowd to feed on Christmas Eve, I often cut the thick swordfish steaks in half horizontally, creating two thinner servings. This is easier to do while the steaks are semi-frozen.

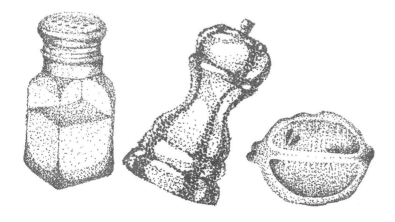

Involtini di Sogliola
Sole Bundles in Marinara Sauce

1 recipe Marinara Sauce (Page 107)
1 pound sole fillets
1 recipe Herb Mixture (Page 81)
Romano or Parmesan cheese, grated (optional)
Fresh basil (optional)
1 package frozen peas, thawed at room temperature (optional)
1/2 pound cooked spaghetti or linguine (optional)
Butter (optional)

Ann Explains...

Anyone who prepares family meals has those occasional late-afternoon flashes during which they realize that they have not thought about dinner. It's then that I do my most creative cooking. Checking my freezer and pantry for provisions, I'm challenged to come up with an impromptu meal based on items at hand. This sole dish resulted from just such a necessity.

Prepare the Marinara Sauce and cook for about 20 minutes. In the meantime, wash the fillets and pat dry. If they are large, cut them into pieces about 2-1/2-inches wide and 4-inches long. Prepare the herb mixture and spread a little on each piece of fish. Roll each, securing with round wooden picks.

When the sauce appears to be fairly thick, set the uncooked fish rolls on the sauce. Cover and cook gently over a medium heat for about 12 minutes, or until the fish flakes easily. Sole is a delicate fish and cooks quickly. Serve the fish rolls with grated cheese. Some fresh minced basil will enhance the flavor of this dish.

If you wish, you may add the peas to the sauce when you add the fish rolls, then serve it as a stew with crusty bread. Another way of serving the sole is over cooked pasta that has been tossed with optional butter and cheese.

Pesce ai Ferri alla Anna
Ann's Broiled Fish and Lemon Sauce

1 pound fish fillets (sole, whitefish, salmon, fresh tuna or swordfish)
3 tablespoons olive oil
2 tablespoons melted butter or margarine
1 large clove garlic, through a press
3/4 teaspoon onion salt, or less, to taste
1/8 teaspoon pepper
1/2 teaspoon each: oregano, basil
1 teaspoon dried parsley flakes
1 teaspoon Worcestershire sauce
1/2 teaspoon A-1 sauce (optional)
Paprika
2 lemons
1 tablespoon minced fresh parsley

Rinse and pat the fish fillets dry. In an oven-proof baking dish that will accommodate the fillets in one layer, combine all the ingredients from the olive oil through the optional A-1 sauce. Mix well.

Place the fillets in the pan, fleshy side down in the marinade, then turn them over. Sprinkle lightly with the paprika and place them in a preheated broiler approximately 3 inches from the source of heat. Broil until the fish is lightly browned and it flakes easily. Thin fillets will cook in 10 to 12 minutes, thicker fillets in 18 to 20 minutes.

Remove from the broiler and squeeze the juice of 1 lemon over the fish, sprinkle on the parsley and serve with pan juices and additional lemon wedges.

Ann's Tips...
This fish may be prepared in your broiler or grilled over charcoal. I find it best to use a hinged, long-handled broiler rack that closes with a clamp when cooking fish outdoors. Coat the rack with a vegetable spray before starting. If you do decide on the outdoor method, choose one of the meatier fishes rather than the sole.

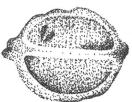

From Ann's Kitchen

Baccalà alla Siciliana
Codfish, Sicilian-Style

2 pounds fresh or frozen codfish
4 potatoes, pared and quartered
1/2 cup olive oil
1 large onion, sliced
2 cloves garlic, through a press
1/2 cup dry white wine
Salt and freshly ground pepper to taste
1 (8-ounce) jar black Italian olives, pitted
2 tablespoons capers
2 tablespoons pine nuts
2 tablespoons golden raisins
2 pounds fresh tomatoes, peeled, seeded, drained and chopped
  or 1 (28-ounce) can, seeded, drained and chopped
2 tablespoons chopped fresh parsley
1 teaspoon basil

Ann Explains...

Baccalà refers to dried salt codfish, which needs to be laboriously soaked over several days to rehydrate it and rid it of excess salt. I find fresh cod to be succulent and sweet, and have substituted it for the salt cod for many years, while retaining the other traditional ingredients in this dish. I hope that purists will forgive me.

Cut the fish into serving pieces, rinse and pat them dry. Cook potatoes in salted water, covered, for 5 to 7 minutes. Drain and reserve the water, which may be added to the casserole if needed for additional liquid.

Put the oil into a large skillet and sauté the onion and garlic until golden in color. Put the cod pieces over the onion-garlic mixture and cover with the wine. Season with salt and pepper and cook until the wine has almost evaporated.

Carefully transfer the fish to a large greased earthenware or glass casserole. Arrange the potatoes between and around the fish. Add the olives, capers, pine nuts and raisins, distributing them over the fish and potatoes.

Cover with the chopped tomatoes and the onion-garlic mixture from the skillet. Sprinkle with parsley and basil and season with additional salt and pepper. Bake in a preheated 350-degree oven for 30 to 35 minutes, or until the fish flakes easily. Halfway through the cooking time, check the casserole to see if additional liquid is necessary.

Verdure e Contorni
Vegetables and Side Dishes

Carciofi Ripieni alla Siciliana
Stuffed Artichokes, Sicilian-Style

6 medium artichokes
Lemons
2 cups bread crumbs mixed with 1/3 cup olive oil
1 large clove garlic, through a press
1/3 cup grated Romano cheese
1/4 cup chopped fresh parsley
1/2 teaspoon each: basil, oregano
Salt and pepper to taste
6 anchovy fillets, chopped

Ann's Tips...

For artichoke lovers, these thistles are a celebration of spring, the season during which they are most abundant. They have a slightly nutty flavor and can be enjoyed in numerous ways. There are many varieties available in Italy, but the two that we are most familiar with in America are the slim, pear-shaped artichoke and the large, round Roman-type, which is very suitable for stuffing. The stuffed artichokes prepared by my mother had a special flavor that she achieved by toasting her bread crumbs in olive oil before adding the other seasonings. She also added a few chopped anchovies.

Remove the outer leaves of the artichokes. Using a sharp knife, trim about 1 inch off of the top, cutting across to make a flat surface. Hold the artichoke by the stalk, push out as many of the small center leaves as possible and scoop out the fuzzy "choke" with the tip of a teaspoon.

Cut a lemon in half and rub the cut surface and center of the artichoke with its juice. Cut the stalks so that the artichokes will stand flat and rub that surface also. Squeeze the juice of the other half of the lemon into a bowl of lukewarm water. Spread the artichoke leaves apart and, using several quick strokes, plunge the artichokes into the water one at a time. Shake off the excess water and stand the artichokes upside down in a colander to drain while preparing the filling.

In a broad-surfaced, heavy skillet put the bread crumbs and oil and combine well by mixing them together with a spoon or your fingers. Place the skillet over a medium heat and stir constantly with a wooden spoon until the crumbs turn a golden brown. Remove from the pan at once as the crumbs will continue to brown if left in a hot skillet. Add the remaining ingredients to the crumbs and combine well.

Pat any excess water from the artichokes using paper towels. Starting with the outer leaves, spread them open and put a little of the crumb mixture in between the leaves. Then start the next row and the next until the artichoke is filled. You do not need to fill the center opening.

In a heavy saucepan with a cover, put an inch of water, a little salt and 2 slices of lemon. Stand the artichokes upright in a pan small enough so that they fit snugly. Bring to a boil over a medium heat, reduce to a simmer, cover and cook for 30 to 40 minutes. If one of the outer leaves comes off easily when pulled on, the artichokes are done.

Asparagi alla Parmigiana
Asparagus Parmesan

1-1/2 to 2 pounds fresh asparagus
5 ounces butter, divided
1 cup fresh coarse bread crumbs
1/2 cup grated Parmesan cheese
1 clove garlic, through a press
1/4 teaspoon each: oregano, basil
Paprika

Ann's Explains...

Another one of the joys of spring is fresh young asparagus. Thomas Jefferson grew asparagus in the greenhouses of Monticello, and as the pioneers traveled westward, they brought this elegant vegetable with them. You may have enjoyed white as well as the wild asparagus, but we are most familiar with the green variety. They are a good source of potassium and Vitamin A. Try to cook fresh asparagus within a few days of purchasing.

Break off the tough ends of the asparagus and wash. Cook in lightly salted water in a large skillet with a cover. Do not overcook. Drain well and attractively arrange in a buttered oblong casserole dish. Dice 2 ounces of the butter into small pieces and place over the asparagus. Melt the remaining butter. Mix the crumbs, cheese and garlic with the herbs. Toss with the melted butter and spread over the asparagus. Dust with paprika before baking in a preheated 350-degree oven until the crumbs are golden brown. Serve at once.

Cook's Note: Fresh coarse bread crumbs are not the same as the dried crumbs used in many recipes. To make them, trim the crusts from several slices of white bread. Cut each slice into strips and leave them out on a bread board for several hours. When they become dry, it will be easy to crumble them coarsely.

Fave al Forno all'Italiana
Baked Beans, Italian-Style

1 large onion, thickly sliced
2 cups sliced celery (diagonal slice, 1-inch wide)
1/4 cup chopped fresh parsley
1/3 cup olive oil
2 (16-ounce) cans butter beans
1 teaspoon basil
1/2 teaspoon oregano
1/2 teaspoon garlic salt, or less, to taste
1/2 teaspoon onion salt, or less, to taste
1/4 teaspoon pepper
6 slices lean bacon
1 tablespoon butter, melted
1/2 cup Seasoned Bread Crumbs (Page 52)
Paprika

Ann's Tips...
You may substitute 1/2 pound of dried fava, lima or broad beans in this casserole. Soak them overnight, then cook them as the package directs. Retain some of the cooking liquid to use in the casserole.

Prepare onion, celery and parsley, keeping each item separate. Heat the oil in a saucepan, add the onion and reduce to low heat. Cover and cook, stirring occasionally, until onions begin to brown slightly. Add the celery and cook an additional 5 minutes, stirring once or twice.

Drain the first can of beans and reserve the liquid. Add the second can of beans and their liquid and the drained beans to the saucepan. Season with the next 5 ingredients and the reserved parsley. Cook very gently for about 20 minutes. Taste and add additional salt if necessary. Cook the bacon until it is half done and remove to a dish. Discard the drippings. Cut the bacon into 1-inch pieces.

Butter an 8-inch-by-11-inch casserole and put half of the beans in it. Place a third of the bacon pieces over the beans, and on top of this pour the remaining beans. Stir the melted butter into the bread crumbs and spread on the beans.

Dot with the remaining bacon pieces, cover with aluminum foil and bake for about 20 minutes. Remove the cover, sprinkle lightly with paprika, and bake uncovered an additional 10 to 15 minutes. If additional liquid is needed, the reserved bean liquid may be spooned in from the corners of the casserole. Serve hot as a side dish. Also good as a buffet or picnic item.

Fagiolini al Pomodoro
Green Bean Casserole

1-1/2 to 2 pounds young tender green beans
1/2 cup Seasoned Bread Crumbs (Page 52)
3 to 4 large firm plum tomatoes, sliced
2 tablespoons grated Romano or Parmesan cheese
1/4 teaspoon each: basil, oregano
2 tablespoons each: olive oil, melted butter

Wash the green beans and remove the tips. Cook in a small amount of salted boiling water until just tender. Do not overcook. Drain the beans well and place in an oblong buttered casserole all laying in the same direction. Sprinkle with bread crumbs. Arrange the sliced tomatoes in rows over the beans and distribute the combined cheese and herbs on them. Combine the oil and butter and pour over all. Bake in a preheated 350-degree oven for 25 to 30 minutes.

Ann's Tips...

Although I like the flavor of green beans and tomatoes together, I'm not overly fond of beans that are drowning in tomato sauce. This makes a nice alternative. You may also try this approach with other green vegetables.

Broccoli alla Parmigiana
Broccoli Parmesan

1 large bunch fresh broccoli, or 2 (10-ounce) packages frozen
1/2 cup fresh coarse bread crumbs (Page 127)
4 tablespoons grated Parmesan cheese
1 small clove garlic, through a press
2 tablespoons butter, melted, and 1 tablespoon olive oil
Paprika

Clean the broccoli, discarding the tough stems and saving all the fresh leaves. Cut the broccoli to make 4- to 5-inch stems. If large, cut in 2 or 3 pieces. Pare the tough surface off the stalk and cut stems into round slices. Wash and cook in lightly salted water to cover for about 15 minutes, or until done. Do not overcook. Drain well. Grease a shallow baking dish and place the broccoli stems and pieces in a single layer. Combine the bread crumbs, cheese and garlic. Toss with the butter and oil and distribute over the broccoli. Bake in a preheated 375-degree oven until it is heated through and the crumbs begin to brown. Sprinkle with paprika and serve hot.

Broccoli con Salsa di Limone
Cold Broccoli with Lemon Sauce

2 bunches broccoli
1 large or 2 medium tomatoes
1/2 cup olive oil
1/3 cup lemon juice
1 large clove garlic, through a press
1/2 teaspoon each: basil, oregano
1/4 teaspoon onion powder
Freshly ground pepper and salt to taste

Ann Explains...

On Christmas Eve, I usually serve this cold broccoli and tomato dish, arranged to look like a Christmas wreath. If cherry tomatoes are available, you can cut them in half and use them to dot the wreath like "berries," instead of placing cut tomato wedges on the plate's border.

Select firm green broccoli and cut into florets. Trim any tough outer skin from the remaining stalks and cut into uniform pieces. It is best to cook them in a broad pan, such as a skillet or Dutch oven with a cover.

Put about an inch of water in the pan, bring to a boil and arrange the broccoli in one layer. Season lightly with salt, cover and cook over a medium heat for 7 to 10 minutes. Watch carefully; do not overcook. The broccoli should be tender enough to pierce with a fork but still firm. While the broccoli is cooking, combine the remaining ingredients to make the lemon sauce. Set aside.

Using a slotted spoon or spatula, remove the broccoli to a round platter arranging in a circular fashion with the florets facing the outer rim. Leave a space in the center to set a bowl with lemon sauce. Cut the tomatoes in wedges and set them around the outer edge of the broccoli. Chill for several hours.

At serving time, put the lemon sauce in a small glass bowl. Set it in the center of the platter with a spoon and serve as a side dish.

Carote al Prezzemolo
Buttered Parsleyed Carrots

1-1/2 to 2 pounds carrots
1/3 cup water
4 tablespoons butter
1/2 teaspoon salt
1/2 teaspoon onion salt, or to taste
1 teaspoon sugar
2 tablespoons chopped fresh parsley
Dash nutmeg (optional)

Pare and slice the carrots into 1/4-inch diagonal slices. If tender new small carrots are available, these may be prepared whole. Put the carrots into a skillet that has a cover, add the water, butter, salts and sugar. Bring to a boil, cover the pan and lower the heat to a simmer. Check occasionally and stir until the carrots are tender and the liquid evaporates. If the carrots are cooked before the liquid evaporates, remove the cover and cook a few minutes longer over a high heat. Taste to check the seasoning and add the parsley and optional nutmeg. Combine well and serve as a side dish.

Ann's Tips...

Use small- to medium-sized carrots for this dish. Large carrots can be woody and lacking in flavor.

Melanzane alla Parmigiana
Eggplant Parmesan

2 medium eggplants
Salt
Oil for frying (corn oil and olive oil, mixed)
Flour
Marinara Sauce (recipe follows)
Grated Romano cheese
Grated Mozzarella cheese
Fresh basil and mint leaves, chopped

Select fresh, firm shiny eggplants with green tops. Wash, then trim a 3/4- to 1-inch-thick slice off the top and bottom of each. Peel the skin if desired and cut into slices about 1/3-inch thick.

Sprinkle the slices with salt and place on a plate in layers between sheets of paper towel. Put a heavy bowl or something else of weight on top and allow to rest for 1/2 hour. Pat dry with paper towels.

Put about 1/2 inch of oil in a large skillet. (Using part olive oil helps in the browning and adds flavor). While heating the oil, dip each slice of eggplant in flour. Shake off excess. Cook over a medium-high heat, turning to brown both sides. Remove and place on a plate lined with paper towels. Add more oil as needed and continue until all the eggplant is cooked.

Prepare the Marinara Sauce, then place a little sauce on the bottom of a glass pie dish or casserole. Add a layer of eggplant, top with some sauce and sprinkle with a little of the Romano and mozzarella cheeses. Dot with basil and mint. Continue layering with eggplant, sauce, cheeses and herbs.

Bake in a preheated 350-degree oven until the casserole is heated through and the cheese is melted. Let stand awhile before serving.

Menu Suggestion

A Delicious Picnic

•

Insalata di Pollo

•

Melanzane alla Parmigiana

•

Fagioli Marinati

•

Pane

•

Melone

•

Vino e Birra

•

Eggplant Parmesan

Marinara Sauce

2 tablespoons olive oil
3 tablespoons minced onion
1 clove garlic, minced
1 (1-pound) can tomatoes
1 (8-ounce) can tomato sauce
2 large basil leaves, chopped, or 1/2 teaspoon dried
2 mint leaves, chopped, or 1/4 teaspoon dried (optional)
1 tablespoon chopped fresh parsley
Salt and pepper to taste

Heat the olive oil in a saucepan, add the onion and cook gently until soft and translucent. Add the garlic and sauté another minute or so. Put the tomatoes in a blender and puree for approximately 3 seconds. Add to the saucepan together with the tomato sauce and seasonings. Cook over a medium heat to thicken slightly.

Ann's Tips...

This dish is good hot, cold or at room temperature, which makes it a good take-along dish for picnics and other outings.

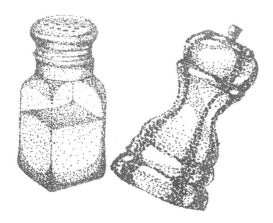

Cipolle Trifolate
Sautéed Onions

6 tablespoons butter
2 tablespoons dry white wine or sherry
2 large or 4 medium onions, thickly sliced
2 tablespoons lemon juice
1/2 teaspoon nutmeg
2 tablespoons chopped fresh parsley
Paprika

Ann's Tips...
These are good served with roasted beef or pork, a turkey dinner or even the humble hamburger.

Heat the butter in a frying pan with the wine or sherry and add the onions. Cook over a medium-low heat, stirring from time to time, until the onions become transparent and begin to brown very lightly. Just before serving, add the lemon juice, nutmeg and parsley and combine well. Put into a warm serving bowl and sprinkle lightly with paprika.

Piselli con Cipolle
Peas with Onions

1 large onion
1 tablespoon water
1/4 cup butter or olive oil
2 (10-ounce) packages frozen peas, defrosted
Garlic salt
Freshly ground pepper
3 tablespoons minced fresh parsley (optional)
Nutmeg

Menu Suggestion

A Birthday Dinner

•

Gamberi Marinati

•

Manzo Brasato

•

Purè di Patate

•

Piselli con Cipolle

•

Torta di Cioccolata

•

Cut the peeled onion into thick slices and put them into a saucepan with the water and butter. Bring to a boil over a medium heat while stirring. Cover and continue to cook, stirring frequently, until the water evaporates and the onions take on a transparent golden color. Add the peas and a little additional water. Season with garlic salt and pepper, cover, and complete cooking. Just before serving, add optional parsley and a light dash of nutmeg. Serve hot.

Peperoni Fritti
Fried Peppers

3 to 4 peppers
1/4 cup olive or salad oil
1 small onion, thickly sliced (optional)
1 small clove garlic, halved (optional)
Salt
Pepper
Basil
Oregano
Red pepper flakes (optional)

Wash, dry and cut the peppers into halves. Remove the seeds and white membrane and cut each half into 1-inch strips. Heat the oil in a skillet over a medium heat, add the peppers and stir to coat with oil. Cook for about 20 minutes while stirring occasionally. If onion and garlic are used, add after the first 5 minutes. (If they are omitted you may want to season with garlic and onion salts instead of the plain salt.)

When the peppers are done, season with salt, pepper, basil, oregano and optional red pepper flakes. Combine well and remove to a serving bowl. May be used hot or cold with Italian sausage sandwiches, hamburgers or as a side dish.

Ann's Tips...
I suggest using the oven method when preparing a large quantity of peppers. When cooking more than 3 or 4 peppers on the stove, you may end up with vegetables that are more steamed than fried.

Variation (Oven Method)

Cut washed and dried peppers in 1-inch strips, and place in a baking pan with sufficient oil to just coat them. Mix the peppers with your hands to ensure an even coating of oil. If you like garlic flavor, you may add several cloves, cut in halves, according to taste.

Place in a preheated 350-degree oven and bake, stirring every 20 to 30 minutes. Peppers are done when they begin to turn brown at the edges. Remove from the oven and season as desired. Onion salt, garlic salt, pepper, red pepper or oregano may be used.

Peperoni Ripieni
Stuffed Peppers

6 medium peppers

1 cup rice

2 cups water

1 teaspoon salt

1/4 cup olive oil

1 medium onion, diced

1 large clove garlic, minced

2 tablespoons minced celery

1 pound ground round steak

2 tablespoons chopped fresh parsley

1 teaspoon basil

1/2 teaspoon oregano or thyme

1 teaspoon onion salt, or less, to taste

1 teaspoon garlic salt, or less, to taste

1/2 teaspoon pepper

1/4 cup grated Romano or Parmesan cheese

2 eggs

Salt

Marinara sauce (recipe follows)

Grated Romano or Parmesan cheese

Ann's Tips...

For a meatless meal, you can substitute 12 ounces of canned tuna for the cooked ground beef in this recipe. Add the drained tuna to the sautéed onion, garlic and celery. Stir in the seasonings and proceed.

Wash the peppers. Cut into halves lengthwise, remove the seeds and pat dry. Put the rice, water and 1 teaspoon of salt into a small saucepan with a cover. Place over medium heat, bring to a boil and reduce heat to simmer. Cover and continue cooking for about 20 minutes, or until all the water is absorbed. Set aside.

Put the olive oil, onion, garlic and celery in a skillet. Place over a medium heat, stirring occasionally, until the vegetables become limp and begin to brown somewhat. Add the ground round and loosen the meat with a wooden spoon so that it spreads in the pan.

Add the next 6 ingredients, then stir and cook until all redness is gone from the meat. If meat other than ground round is used, you may find it necessary to remove some excess fat before combining it with the rice. In a large bowl, combine the rice and meat, then add the cheese and eggs and mix well.

Stuffed Peppers

Oil a large baking pan or casserole in which all the peppers can be arranged in one layer. Place all the peppers, cut-side up, and sprinkle lightly with salt. Spoon the filling into the peppers dividing the ingredients evenly. Spoon some marinara sauce on each pepper and pour the rest around the peppers.

Cover with aluminum foil or a casserole cover, place in a preheated 350-degree oven and bake for 45 minutes. (Thick-skinned peppers may require a longer cooking period, about 1 hour.) Remove the cover, sprinkle each pepper lightly with additional grated cheese, return to the oven and bake an additional 15 minutes uncovered.

Marinara Sauce

1/4 cup olive oil
1 medium onion, diced
2 cloves garlic, minced
2 tablespoons thinly sliced celery
2 tablespoons chopped green pepper
1 (28-ounce) can, or 2 (1-pound) cans tomatoes or tomato sauce
1/2 teaspoon onion salt
1/2 teaspoon garlic salt
1 teaspoon sugar
1/2 teaspoon pepper, or less, to taste
1 teaspoon dried basil
1/2 teaspoon oregano

Ann's Tips...
This sauce may be used for fish, pasta or rice, or with other vegetable dishes.

Put the first 5 ingredients into a saucepan, place over a medium heat and cook, stirring occasionally, until the vegetables become limp and begin to brown. Remove from heat. If using whole canned tomatoes, put them in blender at low speed for a few seconds. Add the tomatoes or tomato sauce to the vegetables in the saucepan, then add remaining ingredients. Combine well and taste for seasoning. No need to cook before adding it to the peppers.

Patate Arrosto
Oven-Browned Potatoes

Ann Explains...

Oven-browned potatoes are a popular side dish when served with any of a number of roasts. They are my favorite, and I serve them in a variety of ways.

5 to 6 medium potatoes, red or Idaho
2 tablespoons olive oil
2 tablespoons butter or margarine, melted
2 tablespoons white wine
1 chicken bouillon cube, or 1 teaspoon bouillon granules
2 cloves garlic, cut in half
Pepper
Rosemary

Peel and cut the potatoes in quarters, wash and pat dry. In a roasting pan, put olive oil, butter, wine, chicken seasoning, garlic, pepper and potatoes. Mix to combine and coat the potatoes evenly. Sprinkle with some rosemary and bake in a preheated 400-degree oven, stirring from time to time. If they are not browning enough, raise the temperature to 450 degrees after 1 hour and bake until they have browned. They may be finished in the broiler if watched closely.

Patate Croccanti
Crispy Golden Potatoes

Ann Explains...

This recipe came to our family table by way of good Sicilian cook Prudence Dispensa. They are a big hit whenever we serve them.

6 large potatoes
1/4 cup flour
1/4 cup grated Parmesan cheese
3/4 teaspoon salt
1/8 teaspoon pepper
1/3 cup butter
Fresh parsley, chopped

Peel the potatoes and cut into quarters or sixths. Combine the flour, cheese, salt and pepper in a bag. Moisten the potatoes with water. Shake a few at a time in the bag, coating well. Melt the butter in a 9-inch-by-13-inch pan. Add the potatoes and bake in a preheated 375-degree oven for 1 hour. Turn once or twice during the baking. When golden brown, remove and sprinkle with parsley. These work out well if baked in a teflon-coated roasting pan.

Purè di Patate
Mashed Potato Casserole

3 pounds red or russet potatoes
6 tablespoons butter or margarine, divided
1/3 cup milk
1/2 cup sour cream
2 tablespoons minced chives or green onions
2 tablespoons minced fresh parsley
3 strips bacon, crisply cooked and crumbled (optional)
1/8 teaspoon nutmeg (optional)
Paprika (optional)

Peel the potatoes and cut into 2-inch pieces. Rinse them in cold water and put in a pan with water to cover. Add a teaspoon of salt, cover and cook over medium heat until a fork pierces them easily. Drain well and return them to the pan.

Add 4 tablespoons of the butter and all the other ingredients except the paprika. Mash or whip until light and fluffy. An electric mixer will help here. (If using bacon, add toward the end of the whipping process). Taste to check seasoning and add salt and pepper if desired.

Grease a 2-quart casserole and put in the mashed potatoes, making peaks on top with the back of a spoon. Cut the reserved 2 tablespoons of butter into small pieces and dot the casserole with it. Sprinkle with paprika if desired. Bake in a preheated 350-degree oven for 20 to 30 minutes, or until heated through. May be made in advance and heated at serving time.

Cook's Note: This manner of preparation is also good for Twice-Baked Potato Boats, using baked potatoes instead of boiled and returning the ingredients to the scooped-out potato shells instead of baking in a casserole.

Ann's Tips...
When entertaining guests, bear convenience in mind. These potatoes can be prepared in advance, freeing your time for other duties and dishes. The casserole can also be brought along to a dinner party to lighten the load of the hostess. During the visit, just place it in the oven before dinner.

Crocchette di Patate
Potato Croquettes

3 pounds Idaho or Russet potatoes, pared and cubed
2 tablespoons butter or margarine
1/3 cup milk
1/4 cup bread crumbs
2/3 cup grated Romano or Parmesan cheese
1 clove garlic, through a press
2 tablespoons minced fresh parsley
1/4 teaspoon nutmeg
2 eggs, beaten
Salt and pepper to taste
3/4 cup bread crumbs
1/4 cup flour
Oil for frying

Ann's Tips...
These may also be prepared as anchovy-stuffed croquettes. To do so, drain a 2-ounce can of anchovies and cut into halves. Form potato mixture into patties and place a piece of anchovy into the center of each. Form each patty into a cylinder and roll in the bread crumb mixture, then proceed as directed.

Place the potatoes in a pan with salted water to barely cover. Cook, draining when a fork pierces the potatoes easily. Return to the pan, mash and whip, adding all the ingredients through the beaten eggs. Check taste and adjust with salt and pepper.

Allow to cool, then form into golfball-sized balls. Combine 3/4 cup bread crumbs with the flour and roll each potato ball in it. Heat about 1/4 inch of oil in a skillet, and when sufficiently hot, add the potato balls without crowding.

Using 2 forks, carefully turn the potatoes to brown on all sides. Remove to paper towels to drain. You may want to wipe the skillet after cooking half of the balls, then finish the rest using fresh oil. This helps to keep all the croquettes a golden brown.

Warm in the oven before serving. These also may be frozen and stored in tightly covered containers. To serve, place in a preheated 350- to 375-degree oven until heated through and crisp.

Patate Fritte con Cipolle
Fried Potatoes with Onions

3 large red potatoes, or 2 large Idaho
1/3 cup corn oil
1 medium onion
2 tablespoons butter or margarine
Onion salt
Pepper
Parsley
Paprika

Pare the potatoes and cut each lengthwise into 3 slices. Cut each slice into 3 strips and each strip into cubes of equal size. Wash and pat them dry with paper towels. Heat the oil in a heavy skillet and cook the potatoes over a medium heat until they are golden. Watch carefully as they cook, turning frequently. Remove with a slotted spoon and drain on paper towels. Meanwhile, cut the onion into thick slices and sauté them in the butter or margarine in a separate pan. Cook gently until tender and starting to color. To serve, toss the potatoes and onions together and sprinkle with onion salt, pepper, parsley and paprika. Serve hot.

Ann Explains…
While it's true that you do your waistline a favor if you eat a plain baked potato, it's just as true that most of us like to eat potatoes embellished with other tasty ingredients. These potatoes have rounded out many a family meal.

Spinaci con Aglio ed Olio
Spinach with Garlic and Oil

2 pounds fresh spinach
3 to 4 tablespoons olive oil
2 large cloves garlic, cut in thirds
Salt and pepper (optional)

Wash the spinach to make sure it is free of sand. Pick over, discarding tough stems and any discolored leaves. Put in a sauté pan or large heavy skillet and cook it with only the water clinging to the leaves. Cook over a medium heat, stirring occasionally, for 5 to 6 minutes, or until the spinach begins to wilt. Drain, if necessary. Add the olive oil to the pan along with the garlic and sauté together until spinach is tender. You may serve with the garlic or discard it. Salt and pepper may be added.

Ann's Tips…
This is a good way to prepare any greens your family enjoys.

Zucchine Ripiene di Carne
Meat-Stuffed Zucchini

2 zucchini, about 9 inches long
3 tablespoons olive oil, divided
1/2 small onion, minced
4 slices Italian bread, crusts removed
1 large clove garlic, minced
1/3 cup grated Romano cheese
2 tablespoons minced fresh parsley
3 large basil leaves, minced
1 large egg
1 teaspoon salt
1/2 teaspoon pepper
1 pound ground round steak
Marinara Sauce (recipe follows)
2 or 3 tablespoons grated Romano cheese

Ann's Tips...
The most desirable zucchini are those that are narrow and small to medium in length. If your garden has gotten away from you and you have some slightly larger ones to use up, you can try stuffing them in this manner.

Lightly scrape the zucchini, cut off the ends and cut each zucchini into 3 even pieces. Put them in lightly salted boiling water to cover and cook for 5 minutes, then drain and cool. Cut each piece in half lengthwise, scoop out the seeds and pulp, chop finely, and set aside. Select a baking pan that will hold the 12 pieces in one layer. Use 1 teaspoon of the oil to grease the pan, then place the zucchini pieces in it.

Heat 2 tablespoons of the remaining oil in a skillet and cook the onion for 3 minutes over a medium heat. Add the zucchini seeds and pulp and cook another 3 minutes. Set aside. Soak the bread slices and squeeze to remove the water. Chop the bread and measure 1/2 cup, well packed. Put in a bowl together with the zucchini mixture and add the garlic, cheese, parsley, basil, egg, salt and pepper. Combine well with a fork. Add the ground beef and work in lightly but well with your hands. Form into 12 oblong portions to fit the zucchini centers and press into the zucchini. Sprinkle with the remaining 2 teaspoons of oil and bake in a preheated 400-degree oven for 25 minutes. Meanwhile, prepare the Marinara Sauce. Pour over the partially-baked zucchini and sprinkle with cheese. Reduce oven heat to 350 degrees and bake another 15 minutes.

Meat-Stuffed Zucchini

Marinara Sauce

3 tablespoons olive oil
1/2 small onion, chopped
1 large clove garlic, minced
2 strips red or green bell pepper, 1-inch wide, chopped
1 (1-pound) can tomatoes, diced
1/2 teaspoon salt
Pepper to taste
1/2 teaspoon sugar
2 tablespoons chopped fresh parsley
4 large basil leaves, chopped

In a medium saucepan, heat the oil and add the onion. Cook for 3 minutes over a medium heat, then add the garlic. Add the pepper and cook another 3 minutes while stirring, then add the tomatoes, salt, pepper and sugar and cook about 15 minutes to reduce liquid. Remove from the heat and add the parsley and basil.

Italian Proverb

"L'appetito vien mangiando."

•

(Appetite comes with eating.)

•

Zucchine al Forno
Baked Zucchini, Italian-Style

4 or 5 narrow zucchini, 8- or 9-inches long
Salt
1 cup flour
1/2 cup plus 1 tablespoon olive or corn oil
1 small onion, minced
1 small clove garlic, minced
1 pound ground beef
Salt and pepper to taste
1 tablespoon parsley, chopped
Pinch oregano
1/2 teaspoon dried basil, or 2 large fresh leaves, chopped
6 tablespoons grated Romano or Parmesan cheese, divided
Marinara Sauce (Pages 68-69)
3 large basil leaves, chopped
3 large mint leaves, chopped

Ann Explains...

This casserole may be prepared a day in advance and refrigerated. Bring to room temperature before baking. Any leftover sauce may be used with other vegetables.

Select firm fresh zucchini no more than 1-1/2- to 2-inches in diameter. Large zucchini are too seedy for this recipe. Lightly scrape skin and wash. Remove ends and cut into diagonal slices, about 1/4-inch thick. Sprinkle the slices lightly with salt, then shake a few slices at a time in a bag containing the flour.

Put 1/2 cup of the oil into a broad frying pan and heat over a medium-high heat. When the oil is sufficiently hot, add zucchini slices after shaking off any excess flour. Brown on both sides and continue until all slices are cooked. Set aside.

Heat the 1 tablespoon of oil, then add the onion and garlic and sauté for 2 or 3 minutes over a medium heat. Add the meat, season with salt and pepper, and add the next 3 ingredients. Continue to cook, stirring occasionally until brown. Drain off any accumulated fat from the meat. Add 2 tablespoons of grated cheese and stir to combine with the meat. Set aside.

Prepare a marinara sauce such as Salsa di Pomodoro or one of its variations (Pages 68-69).

Baked Zucchini, Italian-Style

To assemble, use either an oblong or round oven-proof casserole dish. Layer half of the zucchini slices close together, cover with half of the remaining grated cheese and half of the chopped basil and mint leaves. Add the meat and cover with a little sauce. Make another layer of zucchini slices. Repeat with sauce, cheese and chopped herbs. Bake in a preheated 350-degree oven for about 20 minutes, or until bubbly hot. Allow to stand a few minutes, then serve.

Zucchine Fritte
Breaded Fried Zucchini

4 or 5 medium zucchini
Salt
Flour
2 eggs beaten
1 cup Seasoned Bread Crumbs (Page 52)
1/2 cup olive or corn oil

Lightly scrape the skin and rinse the zucchini. Remove the ends and cut each zucchini into diagonal slices about 1/4-inch thick. Sprinkle the slices with salt and then shake a few slices at a time in a bag containing flour. Shake off excess flour, dip the slices into the beaten eggs, then into the seasoned bread crumbs. Prepare all of the slices before beginning to fry. Heat the oil over a medium-high heat and brown the breaded zucchini slices on both sides. You will need to do this in several batches.

Verdure Miste
Vegetable Medley

1 bunch broccoli, or 1 medium head cauliflower, or combination
4 medium carrots
3 or 4 narrow zucchini
1 large or 2 medium onions, thickly sliced
1/4 cup butter
1 tablespoon dry white wine or water
1/2 teaspoon nutmeg
2 tablespoons chopped fresh parsley
3 tablespoons olive oil
2 cloves garlic, minced
Salt and pepper to taste
2 tablespoons grated Romano or Parmesan cheese

Menu Suggestion

Company's Coming

Antipasti Misti
•
Arrosto di Maiale
•
Patate Croccanti
•
Verdure Miste
•
Pizzelle con gelato
•

Trim the broccoli or cauliflower of tough outer skin and cut into florets. Pare and slice the carrots into 1/4-inch diagonal slices. Scrape the zucchini and slice diagonally. Prepare onion, garlic and parsley, keeping each item separate.

Put the broccoli and/or cauliflower in a sufficient amount of salted water to just cover the vegetables and cook until barely tender. Drain and rinse in cold water to stop the cooking and set aside. Repeat the process with the carrots.

Melt the butter with the wine or the water in a small saucepan and, when hot, add the onions and stir. Cook over a medium-low heat while stirring from time to time until the onions are transparent and are starting to brown lightly. Add the nutmeg and parsley to the onions and set aside.

About 20 minutes before serving, heat the olive oil in a large skillet, add the garlic and cook for a minute. Add the zucchini and stir over a high heat, watching carefully. Do not allow them to overcook.

Reheat the broccoli and/or cauliflower and carrots. (You may use a microwave oven for 2 minutes.) Add them to the zucchini and toss lightly with a large spoon and fork. Add the onion, season with salt and pepper, and heat through. Put in a serving dish, sprinkle with grated cheese and serve hot.

Dolci
Desserts

Cassata alla Siciliana
Sicilian Torte

Pan di Spagna (Sponge Cake)

6 extra large or 7 large eggs, separated
1-1/4 cups sugar
3/4 teaspoon vanilla extract
1 teaspoon grated lemon rind
1 teaspoon grated orange rind
1 tablespoon lemon juice
1/2 teaspoon salt
1-1/2 cups sifted cake flour

Ann Explains...

The elaborate Cassata is served all over Sicily. It is sometimes molded in a bowl with layers of sponge cake and ricotta cream. When unmolded, it is decorated with a confectioners' icing and candied fruits. Sometimes, as in this recipe, it is presented as a layer cake. The decorations and finishing touches here are my own preferences.

Beat the egg yolks in a large bowl until very thick and lemon colored. Gradually beat in the sugar, vanilla, and lemon and orange rinds, mixing well after each addition. Beat in the lemon juice. In another large bowl, beat the egg whites and salt until stiff but not dry.

Pile the egg whites onto the egg-yolk mixture. Sift the flour over the egg whites and carefully fold it into the mixture until all the ingredients are combined. Do not overmix.

Grease the bottom of 2 (9-inch) cake pans, cut wax paper to fit, line the pans with wax paper and lightly butter again. Divide the batter evenly between the 2 pans. Bake in a preheated 325-degree oven for 30 to 35 minutes, or until a toothpick inserted in the center comes out clean. Loosen the cake around the edges and turn it over on a cake rack. Remove the wax paper carefully and allow to cool before assembling.

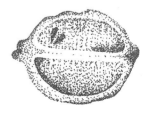

Dolci ❧ Desserts

Sicilian Torte

Pastry Cream

4 large egg yolks
Pinch of salt
1/2 cup plus 2 tablespoons sugar
3 tablespoons flour
1-1/2 cups hot milk
1 square baking chocolate
2 tablespoons chopped walnuts
1 teaspoon vanilla extract
1 teaspoon lemon extract
2 tablespoons maraschino cherries, sliced

In a small mixing bowl, beat the egg yolks with the salt and sugar until thick and very light. Add the flour and beat until smooth. Meanwhile, scald the milk in a saucepan and pour it onto the eggs, stirring briskly. Return the mixture to the saucepan, place on a low heat and stir until it is thickened. Remove from the heat and beat until smooth. Divide the cream, spooning half into a small bowl. To the half remaining in the pan add the chocolate square and melt over very low heat. Stir in the chopped nuts and vanilla. Cover with wax paper and set aside to cool. Add the lemon extract and cherries to the other half of the cream mixture. Stir well and cover with wax paper until ready to use.

Ricotta Filling

1 cup fresh ricotta, drained very well
1/2 cup confectioners' sugar
1/2 teaspoon almond extract
1/2 teaspoon vanilla extract
1/2 teaspoon orange extract
2 tablespoons chopped candied fruit
2 tablespoons diced milk chocolate, or milk chocolate morsels

Menu Suggestion

Save Room for Dessert

•

Minestra di Piselli

•

Cotolette di Vitello

•

Riso alla Anna I

•

Spinaci con Aglio ed Olio

•

Cassata all Siciliana

•

Beat the ricotta with an electric mixer with the confectioners' sugar until smooth and creamy. Add the flavorings, candied fruit and chocolate. Mix well and store in the refrigerator if not using immediately.

Assembly

2 tablespoons Crème de Cacao
2 tablespoons Amaretto
2 tablespoons Anisette

Slice each of the sponge cake layers in half horizontally to create 4 layers. Place the first layer on a cake serving plate, cut-side up, and sprinkle with Crème de Cacao. Spread the chocolate-nut portion of the Pastry Cream on this layer, then cover with a second cake layer, cut-side down. Sprinkle Amaretto on the surface of this layer and spread on the ricotta filling. Cover with the next layer, cut-side up, sprinkle with Anisette and top with the lemon-cherry portion of the Pastry Cream. Cover with the final layer, cut side down, then cover with wax paper and store in the refrigerator until ready to decorate.

Decoration

1-1/2 cups whipping cream
2 tablespoons confectioners' sugar
3/4 teaspoon vanilla extract
Shaved milk chocolate
2 tablespoons toasted slivered almonds
Maraschino cherry and candied fruit pieces

Whip the cream, adding confectioners' sugar as it thickens. Add vanilla extract and whip until it is the desired consistency for spreading on the cake. When the cake is completely covered with whipped cream, circle the top with shaved milk chocolate and almonds. Place a cherry in the middle and add some pieces of candied fruit for color.

Sicilian Proverb

"A tavola si scordano li trivuli."

•

(Troubles are forgotten at the dinner table.)

•

Torta di Mele alla Zia Anna
Aunt Ann's Apple Cake

Cake

2 cups all-purpose flour
1/2 cup sugar
2-1/2 teaspoons baking powder
1/2 teaspoon salt
1/8 teaspoon nutmeg
1 stick butter
1 large egg
1/2 teaspoon lemon extract
Milk
Topping (recipe follows)

Combine all the dry ingredients in a bowl and cut in the butter, using your fingers, until the mixture resembles cornmeal. Break the egg into a 1-cup measure and beat it with a fork. Add the lemon extract and enough milk to fill the cup. Make a well in the flour-butter mixture and pour the liquid into it, mixing until all the dry ingredients have been combined into a soft dough. Divide into 2 (9-inch) buttered pans.

Topping

4 large golden delicious apples, pared and thinly sliced
3 tablespoons each: flour, sugar
1/2 teaspoon cinnamon
3 tablespoons firm butter, cut into tiny squares

Arrange the apples in circles around the cake batter, starting at the outer edge and continuing into the center. Mix the flour, sugar and cinnamon together and spread the mixture over the apples. Dot with the butter. Bake in a preheated 400-degree oven for 35 to 40 minutes.

Cook's Note: Granny Smith can be used instead of golden delicious apples in this recipe. Purple plums are also a tasty substitute.

Ann Remembers...
In memory of my Aunt Anna Ragona, who often made apple cake on the spur of the moment when guests would arrive unexpectedly, I offer my version for this simple recipe. This is a good take-along cake, but it tastes best when served warm.

Torta di Cioccolata
Chocolate Angel Food Cake

Cake

3/4 cup sifted cake flour
4 tablespoons cocoa
1-1/4 cups egg whites (9 to 10 egg whites)
1/4 teaspoon salt
1 teaspoon cream of tartar
1-1/4 cups sifted sugar
1 teaspoon vanilla extract

Sift the cake flour and cocoa together 4 times. Set aside. Beat the egg whites and salt until foamy throughout. Add the cream of tartar and continue beating until the egg whites are stiff enough to hold a peak, but not dry. Gently fold in the sugar, 2 tablespoons at a time, until all is used. Fold in the vanilla. Sift small amounts of the flour-cocoa mixture over the egg whites and fold in quickly but lightly; continue until all the dry ingredients are used. Pour the batter into a 10-inch tube pan and cut through the batter with a spatula to remove large air bubbles. Bake in a preheated 350-degree oven for 50 to 70 minutes, or until a toothpick inserted in the center comes out clean. Invert the pan and let the cake hang in the pan until cool.

Filling

2/3 cup sugar
1/4 teaspoon salt
6 tablespoons flour
2 cups milk
2 egg yolks, beaten
1 tablespoon butter
1/2 teaspoon each: lemon extract, vanilla extract
1-1/2 squares baking chocolate, melted

Combine the sugar, salt and flour in a saucepan and add a small amount of the milk to make a paste. All of the flour should be well blended with no lumps remaining. Gradually add the rest of the milk.

Ann's Tips...

I came up with this chocolate angel food cake back in the 1940s, when I was feeding my baby an egg yolk several times a week. The egg whites were accumulating very quickly, so angel food cakes were making frequent appearances on our table. I decided to dress up my basic recipe for a special occasion, and the result has become a family favorite. We often serve it at birthday celebrations.

Chocolate Angel Food Cake

Stir steadily while cooking over a medium heat until the mixture thickens. Remove from the heat and add a small amount of the hot custard to the beaten egg yolks. Then pour the yolk mixture into the original saucepan and return to the heat. Cook for one or two more minutes, stirring constantly. Turn the heat off and stir in the butter. Pour half of the mixture in a small bowl and add the lemon extract. To the custard remaining in the pan add the vanilla extract and baking chocolate. Cover the custards with wax paper and cool.

Icing

1/2 stick butter, softened
1-3/4 cups confectioners' sugar
1 tablespoon milk, or more, if needed
1-1/2 squares baking chocolate, melted
1/2 teaspoon vanilla extract

Beat the butter and gradually add the sugar and enough milk to make a smooth icing. Stir in the melted chocolate and vanilla. Set aside.

Assembly and Decoration

1/2 pint whipping cream
1 tablespoon confectioners' sugar
1/2 teaspoon vanilla extract
1/3 cup chopped nuts
6 to 8 maraschino cherries, diced
Shaved milk chocolate and cherries for decoration

Whip the cream and add the confectioners' sugar and vanilla. Set aside. Remove the cake from the pan and slice it with a serrated knife into 3 layers. Put the bottom layer on a serving plate, cover it with the chocolate custard and sprinkle with chopped nuts. Place the second layer on this and spread on the lemon custard and diced maraschino cherries. Cover with the third layer. Spread the sides of the cake with the chocolate icing and the top of the cake with the whipped cream. Decorate the border of the cake with chocolate and cherries.

Sicilian Proverb

"Cosi amari, tenili cari cosi duci, tenili 'nchiusi."

•

(Look after sour things carefully, keep sweet things locked up.)

•

Torta di Ricotta Siciliana alla Anna
Ann's Ricotta Torte, Sicilian-Style

Pasta Frolla (Pastry Dough)

3 cups flour
1-1/2 teaspoons salt
1/2 teaspoon baking powder
1 cup cold vegetable shortening, or lard
1 stick cold butter or margarine
1 small egg
1/2 cup orange juice

Ann Explains...

By tradition, certain sweets are reserved for certain feasts. My version of this torta contains all of the flavors I remember from my grandmother's baking, and is always our Easter Sunday dessert. Pasta Frolla is a versatile pastry dough suitable for any type of pie. The recipe listed here will make 4 single-crust pies or 2 double-crust pies. In the context of the Torta di Ricotta recipe, the Pasta Frolla recipe will make a large (9-inch-by-13-inch) torte and a small single-crust pie, or a medium (7-1/2-inch-by-11-inch) torte and a large single-crust pie.

Put the flour, salt and baking powder in a large bowl and stir well. Add the shortening or lard and butter and mix with your fingers or a pie crust mixer until the mixture resembles cornmeal.

Beat the egg with a fork in a small bowl and add the orange juice. Stir well, then pour over the flour mixture and stir together with a fork to combine into a soft dough. You may need to use your hands to finish. Cover the bowl and put it in the refrigerator for at least 1 hour.

About 15 minutes before you are ready to start rolling out the dough, remove it from the refrigerator. Cut the dough in half and, on a well-floured board, roll 1 portion into a 10-inch-by-12-inch rectangle.

Fold the dough into thirds by taking the bottom third and bringing it up to the center of the dough. Then take the top of the dough and bring down over the first 2 layers. Pat the dough down, then turn the dough around so that the narrow end faces you. Turn the dough again into thirds as before. You now have 9 folds in the dough.

Pat the dough down and flour the board and rolling pin again. Carefully roll the dough, adding flour if needed, until you have a 12-inch-by-15-inch-sheet. Fold the dough into thirds and carefully pick it up and set it in the center of a 9-inch-by-13-inch baking dish. Unfold the dough and press it into the baking dish to fit smoothly. If it breaks, you can seal the pieces together. Trim around the edges, leaving an overlap of about 1/4 inch.

Cook's Note: The instructions given here for rolling out the dough are for a large (9-inch-by-13-inch) torte. The recipe may be adapted for a smaller torte. (See Ricotta Filling proportions on next page.)

Ann's Ricotta Torte, Sicilian-Style

Ricotta Filling

Beat the ricotta in a large bowl for about 5 minutes, or until smooth. Slowly add the sugar, butter and extracts. Set aside. In a smaller bowl, beat the eggs until light. Remove 2 tablespoons of the beaten egg, if making a large or medium torte, or 1 tablespoon if making a small pie, and set aside. Slowly fold the beaten eggs into the ricotta mixture, and to this add the chopped candied fruit and the milk chocolate. Use either milk chocolate morsels or diced milk chocolate bars. *(Continued on following page.)*

	Large Torte (9x13 inches)	Medium Torte (7-1/2x11 inches)	Small Pie (9 inches)
Ricotta	3 lbs.	2 lbs.	1 lb.
Sugar	1-1/2 cups	1 cup	1/2 cup
Soft butter	1 stick	2/3 stick	1/2 stick
Almond extract	1 tsp.	2/3 tsp.	1/2 tsp.
Orange extract	1 tsp.	2/3 tsp.	1/2 tsp.
Vanilla extract	1 tsp.	2/3 tsp.	1/2 tsp.
Eggs	6 eggs	4 eggs	2 eggs
Candied fruit	1/3 cup	1/4 cup	2 tbsp.
Milk Chocolate	1/3 cup	1/4 cup	2 tbsp.

Ann's Ricotta Torte, Sicilian-Style

Assembly

3 tablespoons apricot jam
Confectioners' sugar
Cinnamon

Ann Explains...

A touch of cinnamon is a common ingredient in many of our family recipes. The use of this spice is much more prevalent in Sicily than in other parts of Italy. This is due to the Arab influence on the island's history.

Pour the prepared ricotta filling into the pastry-lined baking dish and smooth it out evenly. Cut the remaining dough in half. Roll this half the same as you did the first. After the final folding, roll it into a rectangle as thin as for a pie crust. Using a fluted pie-dough cutter, cut the dough into 1/4-inch strips. Use the strips to make a lattice pattern over the filling. Trim the edges of the torte and press with a fork or make fluted edges.

Mix the beaten egg, which was set aside from the filling, with a little milk. Using a pastry brush, paint the pastry strips with the egg wash. Bake the torte in a preheated 350-degree oven for about 1 hour, or until the crust is golden and the filling has set. If the crust browns too quickly, lower the heat to 325 degrees to finish baking. The filling will rise during baking, then settle when it is cooling.

Remove from the oven and cool on a cake rack. Heat 3 tablespoons of apricot jam over a low heat, breaking it up with a fork. With a pastry brush, paint the entire surface of the torte with the liquefied apricot. Allow the torte to cool completely and, before serving, sprinkle with confectioners' sugar and a light dusting of cinnamon.

Sfinge
Drop Doughnuts

1 package dry yeast
1/4 teaspoon salt
1 teaspoon sugar
1 cup lukewarm water
1-1/2 cups flour
1 egg
1 tablespoon melted butter
Oil for frying
Confectioners' sugar
Cinnamon (optional)

Mix the yeast, salt and sugar in a medium-sized bowl. Slowly add lukewarm water and stir to dissolve yeast. Add half of the flour and beat until smooth. Beat in the egg and melted butter. Add the remaining flour and beat to make a smooth batter. If it is too heavy, add a little more lukewarm water. Cover and allow to rest for about 30 minutes.

In a medium saucepan, heat a sufficient amount of vegetable oil for deep frying. When the oil is very hot, adjust the heat to medium high. Drop the batter by full teaspoons into the hot oil and brown on one side; turn to brown the second side. Remove with a slotted spoon onto cookie sheets lined with paper towels.

These are best served warm or when only a few hours old. Sprinkle with confectioners' sugar and pile pyramid fashion on a plate to serve. If you wish, you may add a final dash or two of cinnamon over all.

Ann Remembers…

Sfinge (or Sfinci) are most often made of a puff pastry similar to the pasta soffiata listed in my recipe for Sicilian Cream Puffs. The main difference is that the sfinci puffs are fried rather than baked. They are soaked in honey and flavored with cinnamon, and are called Sfinci Ammilati. For St. Joseph's Day, these same fried puff pastries are split open and filled with ricotta cream and called Sfinci di San Giuseppe. The Sodaro family has always made a sweet yeast dough fritter that we call Sfinge. My reading tells me that Sfinge is probably from the Arab word "Sfang," which refers to a fried doughnut. If that is true, our version is not far from that tradition. Here is the recipe passed on to me by my cousin Augusta Dugo.

Pasticcini Ripieni
Sicilian Cream Puffs

Pasta Soffiata (Cream Puff Pastry)

1 cup water
1/8 teaspoon salt
1 stick butter or margarine
1 cup flour
4 extra large or 5 small eggs

Ann Explains...

Italians serve cream puffs with a variety of fillings. Sometimes a simple whipped-cream filling is used. Even more popular are flavored ricotta or custard cream. My version combines both of these.

Place the water, salt and butter or margarine into a small saucepan and set it over a medium heat. When the water comes to a boil and the butter or margarine is melted, add the flour all at once and stir vigorously with a wooden spoon until the mixture leaves the sides of the pan and the dough forms into a ball. Continue to cook for another minute or so, remove it from the heat and beat it a few seconds longer.

Put the dough into a large bowl of an electric mixer and, after it has cooled for about 10 minutes, begin beating at a medium speed. Add the eggs one at a time beating for 1 minute after each addition. When the last egg has been added, beat for a total of 5 minutes at a slightly higher speed. Place the mixture in the refrigerator for at least 1 hour.

Grease baking sheets and using a teaspoon, drop the pastry dough onto the baking sheets, placing no more than 4 across the width of the pan. This will make 35 to 40 small puffs. Bake in a preheated 450-degree oven for 15 minutes, then lower the oven to 350 degrees and continue baking for 15 to 20 minutes.

Remove from the oven and cool completely before filling.

Dolci ❧ Desserts

Sicilian Cream Puffs

Ricotta Cream

1 pound ricotta, very well drained
1/2 cup sugar
1/2 teaspoon almond extract
1/2 teaspoon orange extract
1/4 teaspoon cinnamon
1/4 cup chopped candied fruit
1/3 cup diced milk chocolate, or milk chocolate morsels

Put the ricotta in the small bowl of an electric mixer and beat on the slow speed. Gradually add the sugar and flavorings. Raise the speed to medium and beat for about 5 minutes, then remove from the mixer and fold in the candied fruit and chocolate. Store in the refrigerator until needed.

Custard

1-1/4 cups milk, divided
1/4 cup sugar
2 level tablespoons flour
1 level tablespoon cornstarch
2 egg yolks
2 teaspoons butter
1/2 teaspoon vanilla extract
1/4 teaspoon almond extract

Put 1 cup of the milk into a small pan and set over a low heat. Combine the sugar, flour and cornstarch in a small bowl. Add the remaining 1/4 cup of milk and the egg yolks and mix well. When the milk in the saucepan is heated, stir a few tablespoons into the egg mixture and combine well. Then slowly pour the egg mixture into the pan with the remaining hot milk while stirring. Cook over a medium heat, stirring constantly, until the mixture thickens. Turn the heat down to low and cook 1 or 2 minutes longer. Remove from the heat, add the butter and extracts and stir into the mixture. Store in a covered bowl in the refrigerator until ready for use. *(Continued on following page.)*

Ann's Tips...

For a simpler preparation, the cream puffs may be filled with the ricotta cream alone, omitting the custard. However, the combination of the two fillings creates a rich, luscious pastry. If you do omit the custard, you will need 1-1/2 recipes of the ricotta cream.

Sicilian Cream Puffs

Honey Glaze

1 cup honey
2 tablespoons water
Juice of 1/2 orange
Rind of 1/2 orange, grated

Combine all the ingredients in a small saucepan and bring to a slow boil over a low heat. Cook for 2 to 3 minutes. Remove from the heat and cool. Store any unused portion in a covered jar in the refrigerator.

Assembly

Confectioners' sugar
Cinnamon

Using a sharp knife, carefully slice the top off of each puff. Mound a teaspoon of ricotta filling in the bottom half and, if used, 1/2 teaspoon of the cream filling in the top piece, then bring the pieces together. If desired, you may fold the completely cooled Custard Filling into the ricotta mixture, especially if ricotta cheese is unusually dry and mixture appears too heavy.

Set the cream puffs on a serving tray covered with a paper doily. When one layer is completed, lightly drizzle the puffs with the honey glaze, then sprinkle generously with powdered sugar and lightly with cinnamon. Begin a second, then a third layer, building into a pyramid and repeating with the glaze, powdered sugar and cinnamon.

Ann's Tips...

This recipe makes small to medium puffs, but even smaller, miniature cream puffs can be created by using 1/2 teaspoon of pasta soffiata to form them. For large cream puffs, use a tablespoon to drop the dough. Of course, you will need to adjust the cooking time for smaller or larger cream puffs. Whatever size you choose, be sure to allow plenty of space between the puffs when baking. Keep in mind that they will almost triple in volume while baking.

Crostoli
Fried Pastry Ribbons

4 cups flour
2 tablespoons sugar
Pinch of salt
1 (3-ounce) package cream cheese, softened
2 tablespoons oil
3 eggs, beaten
White wine
Oil for frying
Honey
Confectioners' sugar
Cinnamon (optional)

Combine the flour, sugar and salt. Work in the cream cheese as for pie crust together with the oil. Make a well in the center, put in the eggs and 1 tablespoon of the wine and start working into a dough. Add more wine, 1 tablespoon at a time, until the consistency of a firm noodle dough is achieved. Cover and let rest at least 1/2 hour.

Cut the dough in small portions and roll into thin sheets, using a pasta machine if desired. When all the dough is rolled, use a pastry cutter to cut it into strips, about 3-inches-by-1-inch. Make a slit in the center of each strip and draw one end through the slit.

Put a few strips at a time into hot vegetable oil and cook until golden. Remove with a slotted spoon to drain on paper towels. Continue until all are done, putting a paper towel between each layer.

When ready to serve, arrange on a platter. On each layer, drizzle lightly with honey, using the tines of a fork. Sprinkle with confectioners' sugar and optional cinnamon and build on another layer. It is best to do this only with the amount that you plan to serve. The rest will remain crisp for several days if stored dry.

Ann's Tips...

This is another traditional pastry that has almost as many variations as there are Italian cooks. The recipes vary in the types of shortening and the amounts of sugar. Then there is the matter of shape. They can be simply cut into "ribbons" using a fluted pastry cutter, fashioned into bows or tied into knots. For a crispy treat your family will enjoy, roll the pastry very thin. You should almost be able to see light through the dough if you hold it up. And don't skimp on the tasty toppings.

Cannoli alla Siciliana
Sicilian Cream-Filled Shells

Shells

3 cups flour
1/4 cup sugar
1 teaspoon cinnamon
1/4 teaspoon salt
3 tablespoons butter
2 eggs, well beaten
2 tablespoons white wine
2 tablespoons cold water
Beaten egg white
Oil for frying

Ann's Tips...

Be sure to drain ricotta very well before adding it to your recipes. Set it in a colander or sieve for at least 30 minutes if it appears at all watery. Cannoli forms made of metal are readily available in gourmet kitchenware shops, but I remember bamboo or reed-like forms when I was a girl. I've even known some people to use commercial manicotti shells in place of cannoli forms, but the shells are much easier to remove from the metal forms.

Sift the first 4 ingredients together into a bowl. Cut in the butter with a pastry blender until the pieces resemble small peas. Combine the beaten eggs with the wine and water and add it to the flour mixture, a little at a time, until a dough is formed. Turn the dough onto a lightly floured surface and knead until smooth. Cover and chill in the refrigerator for at least 30 minutes.

On a floured surface, roll the chilled dough 1/8-inch thick. Using a 6-inch-by-4-1/2-inch oval pattern made from cardboard, cut out ovals from the dough. Wrap each around a lightly oiled cannoli tube and seal securely using a little beaten egg white.

Fry a few at a time in hot oil until golden brown, being sure not to overcrowd the pan. Be very attentive so they do not burn. Remove from the oil and place on paper towels on a rack to cool. Remove the cannoli tubes and reuse them until all the shells are done. The shells keep well in tightly covered containers.

Sicilian Cream-Filled Shells

Cream Filling

3 cups ricotta cheese, very well drained
3/4 cup confectioners' sugar
1-1/2 teaspoons almond extract
3/4 teaspoon each: vanilla and orange extracts
4 tablespoons chopped candied fruit
6 tablespoons diced milk chocolate, or milk chocolate morsels

Combine the ricotta with the other ingredients and refrigerate until serving time.

Assembly

1/2 cup shelled pistachio nuts
Confectioners' sugar

Put pistachios into 1 cup boiling water. Turn off the heat and allow them to soak for 1 minute. Drain, cool and remove the skins. Allow to dry, then finely chop.

Use a teaspoon to fill the cannoli shells from both sides with the filling. Sprinkle a few chopped pistachio nuts on each end. Dust the cannoli with confectioners' sugar and serve. Do not fill the cannoli shells until just before serving.

Menu Suggestion

St. Joseph's Day Table

•

Olive Schiacciate

•

Peperoni Rossi Arrostiti

•

Finocchi

•

Frittelle di Verdure

•

Frutti di Mare

•

Pasta con le Sarde

•

Frittata di Asparagi e Funghi

•

Fagioli Marinati

•

Pasta e Fagioli

•

Baccalà alla Siciliana

•

Pasta con le Acciughe e Mollica

•

Carciofi Ripieni alla Siciliana

•

Pesce Spada Fritto

•

Sfinge

•

Zeppole di San Giuseppe

•

Cannoli

•

Quaresimali

•

Crostoli

•

Crostata con Panna e Fragole
Strawberry Cream Pie

Crust for Cream Pies

1 cup cake flour
1/2 teaspoon baking powder
6 tablespoons margarine
1 egg yolk
2 tablespoons sugar

Combine the cake flour and baking powder. Cut in the margarine until it is like cornmeal. Beat the egg yolk, mix it with the sugar and work it into the dough. Form into a ball and let rest for a few minutes. Press with your fingers into the bottom of a buttered glass baking dish (8- or 9-inches square). Bake in a preheated 375-degree oven for 18 to 20 minutes. Remove from the oven and let cool.

Cream Filling

1/3 cup sugar
4 tablespoons cake flour
1/4 teaspoon salt
1-1/2 cups whole milk
2 egg yolks
1 tablespoon margarine
1 teaspoon vanilla extract

In a small saucepan, combine the sugar, flour and salt. Slowly mix in a little of the milk, until the ingredients are combined and free of lumps. Continue adding the milk while stirring, place over a medium heat and cook while stirring steadily. When the mixture thickens and comes just to a boil, remove it from the heat. Add a small amount of the hot mixture to the beaten egg yolks, beating well. Add this to the hot custard in the pan, return it to the heat and cook for one or two more minutes, beating continuously. Remove from the heat, add the margarine and vanilla. Mix well, cover with wax paper, and allow to cool. Pour on top of the prepared shell.

Ann Explains...
The year-round availability of fresh produce and fruit has changed our cooking and eating patterns. However, there was a time when fresh, luscious strawberries were strictly a summertime treat, prompting us to call this dessert "Mother's Summer Pie."

Strawberry Cream Pie

Assembly and Decoration

1 pint strawberries
1/2 pint whipping cream
2 teaspoons confectioners' sugar
1/2 teaspoon vanilla extract
Fresh mint leaves

Set aside several whole berries for garnish. Halve the remaining berries and arrange over the cream filling. Chill thoroughly.

Just before serving time, whip the cream with an electric beater. Add the sugar and vanilla and continue whipping until the cream stands in peaks. Spread over the strawberries and garnish with more berries, and fresh mint leaves.

Ann's Tips...
This pie may be prepared with fresh sliced peaches instead of berries.

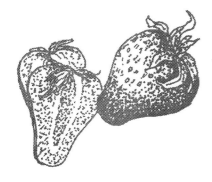

From Ann's Kitchen

Cucciddati
Sicilian Christmas Pastries

Filling

1 pound light figs
1 (8-ounce) jar glazed fruit
Rind of 1 orange, grated
1 pound golden raisins
1/2 cup orange marmalade, or more, as needed
1/2 cup orange juice
1/2 cup toasted filberts, chopped
1/2 cup toasted almonds, chopped
6 ounces chopped milk chocolate or milk chocolate morsels
2 ounces whiskey or brandy
1 teaspoon rum flavoring (optional)

Cut off the hard ends of the figs and grind them with a food chopper or cut them finely with a sharp knife. Next, grind or chop the glazed fruit. Put the figs, glazed fruit and grated orange rind into a large bowl. Into a separate bowl, pour 2 cups of boiling water over the raisins and let rest for 10 minutes. Drain the raisins well, pat dry and add them to the prepared fruit. Bind the ingredients together by adding marmalade and orange juice. If needed, add more marmalade until the consistency is right for holding together. Add the remaining ingredients. Mixture is ready for use.

Pastry

3 cups unsifted all-purpose flour
1/2 teaspoon baking powder
1-1/2 teaspoons salt
1 cup shortening
1 stick butter or margarine
1 small egg
1/2 cup orange juice

My grandmother, Christina Sodaro, made her Cucciddati in horseshoe shapes about 6 inches across and 2 inches wide. These were cut into individual slices at serving time. Her filling was enclosed in a cookie dough. In our home, we have come to prefer pastries made into individual ravioli-sized portions, thus eliminating unused slices, which tend to dry out. Also, I usually substitute a flaky pastry for the cookie dough, which is another family preference.

Sicilian Christmas Pastries

Stir the first 3 ingredients in a bowl. Cut in the shortening and butter or margarine until the mixture is crumbly. Beat the egg, add the orange juice to it, then add to the flour mixture all at once. Mix well and pat the surface with additional flour. Let stand 5 or 10 minutes. Chill in the refrigerator for at least 1 hour.

This recipe is high in shortening content and must be worked carefully. Use a well-floured board and rolling pin, adding more flour as needed. Divide the dough into 4 portions. Roll each portion out into a circle 1/8-inch thick, then fold into thirds. Turn the dough and fold into thirds again. You will now have 9 layers in your pastry dough. Flour the board again and roll the pastry into a thin sheet.

Place the filling on the dough by teaspoonfuls, starting about 3 inches from the top of the pastry, leaving about 1 inch of space between each spoonful. Turn the top of the pastry over the filling and press your finger between each mound of filling. Using a pastry cutter, cut the pastry and press the edges together to be sure the filling is enclosed. Reuse any pastry scraps and continue until it is all used up. Store the remaining filling in a tightly covered container in the refrigerator.

Place pastries on lightly greased cookie sheets and bake in a preheated 425-degree oven for 12 to 15 minutes, or until golden brown. Remove from the oven and let cool.

Icing and Decoration

2 eggs
1 rounded tablespoon soft shortening
Dash salt
Sifted confectioners' sugar
1 teaspoon lemon extract

Beat eggs with shortening and salt, using a fork or wooden spoon. Add sifted confectioners' sugar a little at a time until the icing is the right consistency for spreading. Add lemon extract. Ice each pastry with a pastry brush or knife. Decorate with chocolate shots, chopped nuts, cinnamon, shaved milk chocolate or colored sugars. *(Continued on following page.)*

Ann Remembers...

When making the filling, my grandmother used a heavy, syrupy substance to bind the ingredients. This was called vino cotto, which means "cooked wine." It was made from new white wine of the muscatel grape combined with sugar and cooked until it was condensed into a heavy syrup. Since wine making is no longer feasible for most families, I have not known anyone to make vino cotto for decades. Using all the ingredients Grandma Sodaro used with the exception of the vino cotto, I have devised a recipe for the filling that works very well. It is moist, and keeps for up to a year when stored in tightly sealed jars in the refrigerator.

Pasta per Biscotti (Cookie Dough)

1 stick butter or margarine
2/3 cup sugar
1 teaspoon vanilla extract
1/2 teaspoon almond extract
1/4 teaspoon salt
3 large eggs
1 tablespoon baking powder
3 cups flour

Ann Explains...

The beginning of this recipe contains the flaky pastry dough as I make it. Here, I am including Pasta per Biscotti, the cookie dough that Grandma Christina used with this filling.

In a large bowl of an electric mixer, cream the butter or margarine with the sugar until light and fluffy. Add the flavorings and salt, then the eggs, one at a time. Beat well after each addition.

Combine the baking powder with 2 cups of the flour and slowly add to the creamed mixture. Gradually add about 1/2 cup of the additional flour to the mixture in the bowl, or until it becomes too heavy for the beaters. Remove from the electric mixer and add the remaining flour by hand, mixing until the dough is smooth. Cover and allow to rest for about 10 minutes.

Roll out the dough and follow the directions on the previous page for adding the filling and sealing the cookies.

If desired, cookies can be made by breaking off pieces of dough the size of a large walnut. Roll into 3-inch circles, place 1 teaspoon of filling in the center, fold over, seal and trim.

Horseshoe shapes may be made by rolling the dough long and narrow and spreading the filling down the center. Fold from top to bottom, seal edges, then lift from the top and fold once again over the sealed edge. Form into a horseshoe, seal and trim the tips.

Place cookies on greased cookie pans about 1 inch apart. Bake in a preheated 350-degree oven for 20 to 25 minutes, or until nicely browned. Cool on racks then ice and decorate.

Bocconcini Dolci
Sweet Morsels

1/3 cup toasted coconut
1/3 cup toasted almonds, chopped
1/3 cup milk chocolate morsels
2 sticks butter
1/2 cup confectioners' sugar
1 egg
1/2 teaspoon almond extract
1/2 teaspoon vanilla extract
2 cups flour
Additional confectioners' sugar
Cinnamon (optional)

Preheat the oven to 300 degrees. Spread the coconut on a baking sheet and place it in the oven. Turn several times to prevent burning. When golden in color, remove it and let it cool. Crush the toasted coconut with your fingers. Set aside.

Raise the oven temperature to 350 degrees. Soak the blanched almonds in hot water for 15 minutes. Drain and toast in the oven as with the coconut. When golden, remove, cool and chop. Measure the milk chocolate morsels and set aside.

Beat the butter until creamy. Add the confectioners' sugar and continue beating until light. Add the egg and extracts and beat another minute. Add the flour a little at a time until it is all incorporated. Mix in the coconut, almonds and milk chocolate morsels with a spoon until they are well combined.

Drop the mixture by the teaspoon onto ungreased cookie sheets about 1 inch apart and bake in a preheated 350-degree oven for 15 to 18 minutes. It is best to change the position of the pan from the lower to the upper shelf of the oven after 8 minutes.

Cool completely. Roll in confectioners' sugar. Before serving, sprinkle with a light dusting of confectioners' sugar and, if desired, cinnamon. These may also be rolled into finger-size cookies.

Ann Explains...
I created this recipe using many of my family's favorite flavors. It was originally dubbed the "Best of Everything" cookie.

Biscotti di Natale
Christmas Cookies

Ann Remembers...

As Christmas approaches, our thoughts go back to earlier times and what they meant to us. During the holidays, we were surrounded by grandparents, parents and a host of other relatives who came and went constantly, creating a buzz of activity. We also remember the sights and smells of Christmas. The aromas seemed much more vibrant then: the fragrance of the pine tree being set up near Uncle Tony Sodaro's 8-foot Nativity scene in his home on Loomis Street, the sweet smell of seasonal fruits, and tantalizing aromas of chestnuts roasting on the back of the wood stove, enticing smells from simmering pots, and cookies baking in the oven. These are the things that our memories are built upon, and that inspire us to create similar memories for our own families.

1 stick butter or margarine
2/3 cup sugar
1/8 teaspoon salt
3 eggs
1/2 teaspoon anise seed
1/2 teaspoon each: almond extract, vanilla extract, lemon extract
2-1/4 cups flour
2-1/2 teaspoons baking powder
1/3 cup chopped toasted almonds
1/4 cup chopped candied fruit
Icing (recipe follows)

In a mixer, cream the butter or margarine. Add the sugar and salt and mix until light and fluffy. Add the eggs one at a time beating well after each addition. Add the anise seed and extracts. Turn the mixer to slow speed and add 1 cup of flour and the baking powder. Mix until blended. Slowly add another cup of the flour and blend well with a spoon. Mix the nuts and candied fruit with the remaining 1/4 cup of flour and add to the mixture. Cover the dough and refrigerate for at least 1 hour.

Grease a 15-1/2-inch-by-10-inch cookie sheet. Form 3 parallel loaves lengthwise on the pan. Do this by dropping overlapping teaspoonfuls of dough the length of the pan. Flatten the surface and sides of the loaves with a knife blade. Bake in a preheated 350-degree oven for about 25 minutes, or until golden brown. Cool for about 5 minutes.

Icing and Decoration

1 cup confectioners' sugar
1 tablespoon cocoa
2 tablespoons milk
1 teaspoon butter
1/2 teaspoon anise extract
Multicolored candy shots

Sift confectioners' sugar together with cocoa. Heat the milk with the butter and add to the cocoa mixture together with anise extract. Mix until smooth, then spread over the cookie loaves and sprinkle with multicolored candy shots. Let stand for about 10 minutes. Cut into diagonal slices using a very sharp knife. After 30 minutes, store in tightly covered cookie tins.

Biscotti di Regina
Sesame Seed Cookies

1/2 cup water

4 teaspoons wine

2-1/2 cups shortening

2-1/2 cups sugar

4 eggs

1/2 teaspoon salt

2 heaping teaspoons baking powder

8-1/2 cups flour, or more, if needed

Orange juice

2 cups sesame seeds

Mix the water and wine and set aside. Beat the shortening, add the sugar and beat well. Add the eggs, salt, baking powder and beat well. Add the wine and water.

Add enough flour to form a firm dough and mix well. Chill the dough for 30 minutes. Roll into finger-shaped rods. Dip into the orange juice and then into the sesame seeds.

Bake on greased cookie sheets in a preheated 350-degree oven for 18 minutes, or until lightly golden on the bottom. Turn the cookies over and return to the oven for an additional 2 or 3 minutes.

Ann Explains…

Marge Tolitano is an excellent cook with a special knack for baking. Each Christmas she delights in preparing tray upon tray of delicious cookie gifts for her family and friends. I enjoy making Marge's recipe for this traditional sesame seed cookie. Some Sicilian recipes for Biscotti di Regina call for the addition of 1/2 to 1 teaspoon of cinnamon when mixing the dough.

Quaresimali
Chocolate Spice Cookies

4 cups flour
1-1/2 cups sugar
1/2 cup cocoa
2 tablespoons instant coffee
1/2 teaspoon nutmeg
1/2 teaspoon cinnamon
1/2 teaspoon cloves
1 tablespoon baking powder
1-1/2 sticks margarine
1 cup milk
2 eggs
1/2 teaspoon each: almond, lemon, orange extracts
1 cup broken walnuts or chopped toasted almonds
Icing (recipe follows)

Ann Explains...

These cookies have been a Christmas tradition in our family for many years. However, my dear friend, Giuliana Castellani Koch, instructs me that these are a Lenten cookie. "Quaresima" in Italian means Lent. I hope you enjoy them, whatever time of year you try them.

Put the first 8 ingredients in a large bowl and stir until all the ingredients are well blended. Add the margarine and work with your fingers until a crumbly mixture, resembling cornmeal, is achieved.

Make a well in the center and add all the other ingredients. Stir with a large wooden spoon to combine and dampen all the ingredients. The dough will be sticky. Cover it and refrigerate for 2 to 3 hours.

Scoop by the teaspoonful or shape into balls and place on a greased cookie sheet about 1-1/2 inches apart. Bake in a preheated 375-degree oven for about 10 minutes. Remove them from the cookie sheet to cool on racks. When all are cool, line them very closely on wax paper.

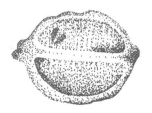

Chocolate Spice Cookies

Icing and Decoration

Hot milk or water
3 cups sifted confectioners' sugar
1-1/2 teaspoons anise extract
Chocolate shots (optional)

Slowly mix hot milk or water with sifted sugar until the frosting is spreadable. Stir in the extract and ice cookies with a pastry brush. If desired, sprinkle them with the optional chocolate shots before the icing dries.

Variation

These may be baked into long narrow loaves (like biscotti) then iced and sliced. On greased cookie sheets, drop overlapping teaspoonfuls of dough in long narrow rows. Smooth out the tops and sides of the loaf. Be sure to keep the loaves narrow, no more than 1-1/2 inches, as they will spread. Bake in a preheated 375-degree oven for 15 to 18 minutes. Remove them from the oven and cool for about 10 minutes, then spread with the icing and sprinkle with the chocolate shots. Slice diagonally and, when the icing is completely dry, store them in tightly covered containers.

Italian Proverb

"Un pane e un anno,
presto se ne vanno."

•

(A loaf of bread and
a year go quickly.)

•

Dodo
Chocolate Drop Cookies

8 cups flour

3-2/3 cups sugar

2 teaspoons cinnamon

2 teaspoons cloves

1-1/2 teaspoons nutmeg

2 teaspoons allspice

2 teaspoons baking soda

3/4 cup cocoa

1 teaspoon salt

2 cups milk

1/2 pound shortening or margarine

1 cup nuts (optional)

Ann Explains...

The chocolate and spice combination is popular, appearing in many variations. This one was handed down to Angela Giunta from her husband Joe's family.

Sift the dry ingredients together. Heat the milk until very warm and melt the shortening in the milk. Let it cool and add to the dry ingredients. Add the nuts if desired. Roll into 1-inch balls and bake in a preheated 375-degree oven for about 12 minutes.

Frosting

2 cups confectioners' sugar

Milk

2 teaspoons anise or vanilla extract

Mix confectioners' sugar with enough milk to make the icing spreadable. Mix in anise or vanilla extract and frost cookies.

Pizzelle
Star Wafer Cookies

1-1/2 sticks butter, very soft
3 eggs
3/4 cup sugar
1-3/4 cups flour
1 teaspoon baking powder
2 teaspoons vanilla
1 teaspoon anise, lemon or orange extract
Confectioners' sugar

Ann Explains...

I have a dozen recipes for Pizzelle but this is the one that draws "ahs" from our crowd. Thanks to Linda Baron for passing along Angela Giunta's recipe.

Beat the butter with the eggs and sugar. Gradually add in the dry ingredients and flavorings. Drop by the tablespoon onto the center of an electric pizzelle iron, close cover and cook only a few minutes. When golden, carefully lift each pizzelle from the iron and place flat on a wire rack to cool. They may also be rolled while still warm, if desired. Store airtight. At serving time, they may be sprinkled with confectioners' sugar.

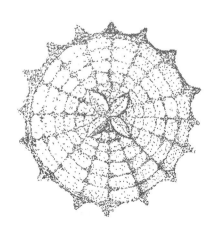

Piatto di Frutta d'Estate
Summer Fruit Plate

Menu Suggestion

A Summer Buffet

•

Insalata Caprese

•

Insalata d'Arance alla Siciliana

•

Caponatina

•

Salsiccia Casalinga

•

Peperoni Fritti

•

Patate Fritte con Cipolle

•

Panini

•

Piatto di Frutta d'Estate

•

1 pint ripe strawberries
3 large ripe peaches
Juice of 1 lemon
3 bananas, not overripe
2 cups fresh pineapple cubes, or canned and drained
1 medium cantaloupe
1 honeydew melon
1/2 cup blueberries
Fresh mint sprigs
Leaf lettuce, washed and dried
1 pound ricotta, very well drained, or cottage cheese (optional)
Ann's Apricot Dressing (optional) (recipe follows)

Wash and dry the strawberries on paper towels. Prepare the peaches by dipping them into boiling water for a few seconds, dropping them into cold water, then peeling off the skin. Cut the peaches in half. Dip each half in lemon juice and set aside. Peel and cut the bananas into 1-inch slices and toss them with the remaining lemon juice. Set aside.

Cut the pineapple and melons into cubes. Wash and dry the mint sprigs and blueberries. Fill the cavities of the peaches with blueberries.

Arrange the lettuce on a large round serving dish, leaving the center free for a small glass serving bowl. Start arranging all the fruit in sections using mint leaves to divide each group. Fill the glass bowl with drained ricotta, cottage cheese or Ann's Apricot Dressing.

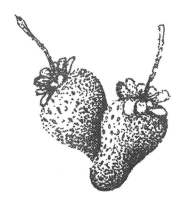

Summer Fruit Plate

Ann's Apricot Dressing

3 tablespoons sugar
1 tablespoon plus 1 teaspoon cornstarch
1 tablespoon lemon juice
3/4 cup apricot nectar
Rind of 1/2 lemon, grated
1/4 teaspoon yellow mustard
1 egg yolk, beaten
1 tablespoon butter or margarine
1 egg white, stiffly beaten
Pinch of salt
1/4 cup sour cream
Mint sprigs and strawberries for garnish

In a small saucepan combine the sugar and cornstarch. Stir in the lemon juice and a small amount of the apricot nectar to completely dissolve the dry ingredients.

Add the balance of the nectar, then cook over a medium heat, while stirring, until the mixture thickens. Stir in the grated lemon rind and the mustard.

Beat the egg yolk, add 1 tablespoon of hot mixture to the egg yolk, then add it to the mixture in the pan and cook another minute or so. Beat in the butter or margarine.

Beat the egg white together with a pinch of salt until stiff. Add 1 table-spoon of the hot mixture to the egg white and fold in. Continue to fold in the balance of the mixture until all is incorporated. Fold in the sour cream and cool in the refrigerator.

Ann's Tips...

For an attractive touch, present this sauce with a sprig of mint and one strawberry in the center.

Pesche al Vino
Sliced Fresh Peaches in Sweet Wine

1 ripe fresh peach per person (preferably Elberta peaches)
Sweet wine
Grated lemon rind for garnish (optional)

Drop the peaches into boiling water for 30 seconds, remove at once and let cold water run on them. Remove the skins. Slice each peach into an individual serving dish and cover with sweet wine. If you wish, you may use your fancy crystal stemware for this. Set in the refrigerator until the peaches and glasses are frosty cold. Sprinkle with some grated lemon rind if desired. Little squares of plain cake or butter cookies may be served with this.

Ann Explains...

Each fall, my mother made a sweet muscatel wine that appeared on our table frequently throughout the year. One of the ways my father enjoyed this homemade wine was with chilled summer fruits. You may try this refreshing dessert with any sweet wine that you enjoy.

Frutta e Formaggio
Fruit and Cheese

Choose the best apples and pears available, allowing 1 or 2 pieces of fruit per person. Serve at room temperature with Gorgonzola, Fontina, Bel Paese, provolone or any other cheese that pleases you. You may slice the fruit before bringing it to the table or, less formally, provide each guest with a fruit knife and fork. If you wish, you can serve a fine port to complement this course.

Caffè Corretto
Italian Brandied Coffee

Italian Proverb

"Il caffè dev'essere caldo come l'inferno, nero come il diavolo, puro come l'angelo e dolce come l'amore."

•

(Coffee must be hot as an inferno, black as the devil, pure as an angel and sweet as love.)

•

For each serving, place 1 sugar cube into a cup, add a twist of lemon peel and 1 jigger of brandy, then fill with very hot coffee. Stir and serve. For best results, coffee should be strong.

Indice
Index

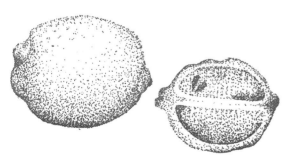

G

H

I

L

P

Q

R

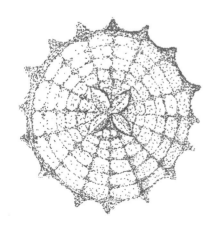

S

W

Z

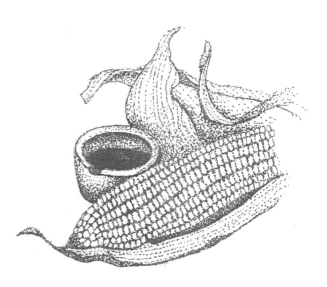

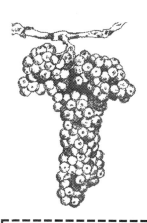

To Order Additional Cookbooks
From Ann's Kitchen

Please send me _____ copies of "From Ann's Kitchen" at $15.95 per cookbook.
I have enclosed $2 for shipping and handling per book.

_____ Cost for book(s). (Number of copies times $15.95)
_____ Cost for S. & H. (Number of copies times $2)
_____ TOTAL COST

Name _____
Address _____
City/State/ZIP_____
Home Phone _____Work Phone _____

Prepayment by check is required. Make your check payable to Fra Noi and
mail it to Fra Noi Cookbook, 3800 Division St., Stone Park, IL 60165.

Please send me _____ copies of "From Ann's Kitchen" at $15.95 per cookbook.
I have enclosed $2 for shipping and handling per book.

_____ Cost for book(s). (Number of copies times $15.95)
_____ Cost for S. & H. (Number of copies times $2)
_____ TOTAL COST

Name _____
Address _____
City/State/ZIP_____
Home Phone _____Work Phone _____

Prepayment by check is required. Make your check payable to Fra Noi and
mail it to Fra Noi Cookbook, 3800 Division St., Stone Park, IL 60165.

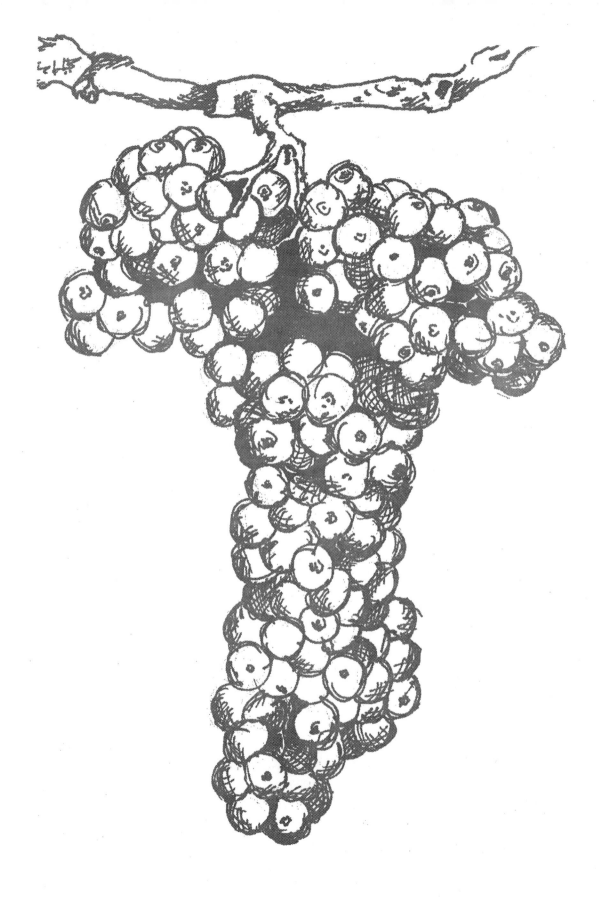